The Anxious-Avoidant Trap

Overcome the push & pull of different attachment styles in your relationship & build lasting connection

Annie Tanasugarn, PhD

New Harbinger Publications, Inc.

Publisher's Note

This publication is designed to provide accurate and authoritative information in regard to the subject matter covered. It is sold with the understanding that the publisher and author is not engaged in rendering psychological, financial, legal, or other professional services. If expert assistance or counseling is needed, the services of a competent professional should be sought.

NEW HARBINGER PUBLICATIONS is a registered trademark of New Harbinger Publications, Inc.

New Harbinger Publications is an employee-owned company.

Copyright © 2025 by Annie Tanasugarn
New Harbinger Publications, Inc.
5720 Shattuck Avenue
Oakland, CA 94609
www.newharbinger.com

All Rights Reserved

Cover design by Sara Christian

Acquired by Elizabeth Hollis Hansen

Edited by Marisa Solis

Library of Congress Cataloging-in-Publication Data on file

Printed in the United States of America

27   26   25

10   9   8   7   6   5   4   3   2   1   First Printing

To the teachers,
Who called on me as the kid in the back of the class
And helped give me a voice;
And to my mentor,
Who always had a wise fishing story to tell
About the one that got away;
I thank you all.

Contents

	Introduction	1
Chapter 1	How Attachment Insecurities Develop	7
Chapter 2	The Three P's of Attachment Insecurity	13
Chapter 3	What's Your Attachment Style?	35
Chapter 4	Insecurities in the Anxious-Avoidant Trap	47
Chapter 5	Exploring Basic Safety Needs	75
Chapter 6	Unpacking Basic Belonging and Esteem Needs	91
Chapter 7	Identifying Common Behavior Patterns	119
Chapter 8	Establishing and Maintaining Intimacy	131
Chapter 9	Fostering Connection and Resolving Differences	157
	References	175

Introduction

Congratulations on taking a positive step in helping empower yourself and your romantic relationship! By learning how to explore your and your partner's unique attachment styles with the tools provided in this book, you can begin to shed light on the dynamics that may be impacting the quality and stability of your relationship. Because your romantic relationship is one of the most intimate relationships you will encounter, it can feel especially stressful if something goes sideways within it. Luckily, this book has been written with both you and your partner in mind to help each of you unpack any attachment insecurities that may be influencing how you approach your relationship.

To start, let's define a few important terms you'll encounter in this book. *Attachment theory* is the lens used to examine behaviors that are specific to a person's unique *attachment style*. Attachment style can be defined as *categorical* or *dimensional*. Categorical approaches label a person's attachment style into specific categories, such as "secure" or "anxious," depending on their behavior patterns. *Dimensional approaches* identify a person's attachment style along an *attachment continuum*. Dimensional approaches in attachment theory allow for more nuance, whereby a person may be higher in some specific traits and lower in others. For example, someone with a more overall *secure attachment* style exhibits higher levels of trust toward others, has firm boundaries, and is more easily able to communicate their needs and vulnerabilities. Yet, this should not suggest that since they are higher in these secure traits that they should be higher in *all* secure traits. This person may still display some insecurities in certain conditions or contexts.

On the flip side, someone with a more *anxious-ambivalent attachment* style or *dismissive-avoidant attachment* style has typically experienced ruptures in their early relationships that have left emotional and behavioral gaps in how they relate to others. Throughout this book, the terms "anxious attachment style" and "avoidant attachment style" will be used for convenience. The emotional and behavioral gaps seen in insecure attachment styles affect how a person relates to others. These are called *attachment wounds* or *attachment insecurities*.

For example, if you are someone with a more anxious attachment style, you may be called "clingy" by your partner. You may insist on spending more time with your partner, or insist on contacting your partner when not with them. With a more anxious attachment style, you may be hypervigilant in looking for inconsistencies in what your partner says and does, or in seeking emotional reassurance from them or others. You may also struggle with feelings of inadequacy, become reactive during conflict, or believe that your partner will eventually abandon you for someone else.

These behaviors resonate with *pulling toward* another, or seeking validation, comfort, and reassurance. When examining attachment along a continuum, there are variances in behavior patterns, including when these behaviors are displayed and in what contexts. However, your overall way of responding will be consistent with a more anxious attachment style.

Contrarily, if you are someone with an avoidant attachment style, you may be unable to trust or depend on others in your time of need, appear hyperindependent, struggle to identify or label your feelings, and tend to shut down during conflict. These behaviors resonate with *pushing away*, or seeking space, autonomy, and distance in order to feel less overwhelmed. As with other attachment styles, there are variances in avoidantly attached behavior patterns, including when these behaviors are displayed and in what contexts. Yet, your overall way of responding will remain relatively consistent with a more avoidant pattern.

Your unique attachment style is based on many lived experiences, including your earliest relationships with your primary caregivers and their ability to have provided you with sufficient love, attention, comfort, and a sense of safety. Attachment style is also influenced by your environment, societal norms, socioeconomic factors, and early adverse experiences. All of these experiences can influence the type of attachment style you develop and how you engage in your relationship with your partner. It's not uncommon to feel more securely attached in some areas of your life while feeling less secure in others.

Finally, it's important to understand what a *push-pull dynamic* is. Simply put, a push-pull dynamic can affect any relationship but is most commonly noticed among romantic couples with opposing attachment styles, especially one anxiously attached partner and one avoidantly attached partner. Together, these two opposing attachment styles create an *anxious-avoidant trap* whereby unhealthy patterns repeat within the relationship, leading to a stalemate in communication, difficulty meeting each other's emotional and relational needs, and misunderstandings between partners.

The more intimate the relationship, the greater the possibility that a stressor will impact the quality of that relationship. Hence, a push-pull dynamic can include differing needs for intimacy, opposing needs for autonomy versus dependence, differences in coping with stress, and contrasting communication styles—leading to unhealthy patterns that reinforce and maintain an anxious-avoidant trap.

How This Book Can Help You and Your Partner

To get the most out of this book, you do not need a formal background in psychology, human development, or attachment theory. It is also not required that you currently be in a romantic relationship. If you are single, you can use your most recent romantic relationship as a guide. All that is required is a desire to more deeply understand yourself, your partner, and how each of your lived experiences may be highlighting or overshadowing certain patterns within your relationship. You should also be open to exploring what may be negatively influencing your relationship.

This book will unpack how the concept "love = pain" is learned from attachment insecurities. It will also explore *safety needs* and *belonging and esteem needs*, all of which are among our most fundamental human needs. The needs to feel safe and as if you genuinely belong can be deeply affected by a more insecure attachment style, which can negatively impact your overall esteem and the quality of your relationships.

You'll be introduced to several types of patterns commonly seen within an anxious-avoidant trap, including fear of intimacy, differences in communication styles, and core insecurities. Moreover, you will learn how to overcome these insecurities within your relationship. You'll discover ways to deepen three types of intimacy. You'll also gain some practical tools that you and your partner can use to strengthen communication and resolve relationship differences.

It is important to recognize that while this book offers tools to support a richer and deeper connection between you and your partner, there are some limitations. First, this book was written to support couples in an anxious-avoidant dynamic. Hence, the exercises and tools in this book are geared toward a relationship wherein one partner is more anxiously attached and the other, more avoidantly attached.

Second, this book is not suited for anyone experiencing an abusive relationship. If you believe that you are in a toxic relationship, it is recommended that you find a safe way to leave, as these relationships cannot be mended.

Third, in order to gain a more intimate connection with your partner, it is recommended that both you and your partner provide consistent dedication in exploring what works best for each of you. This means that both you and your partner actively engage in the different activities, including self-checklists, multiple-choice quizzes, journaling prompts, and the relationship-skills-building practice exercises at the end of each chapter. This commitment becomes an even more important point to drive home during times of stress or conflict, as it can be easier to throw in the towel and revert back to each of your comfort zones.

Because self-help tools can play a significant role in both personal and relational development, they can also foster self-awareness, provide hope and self-reflection, and help you to recognize and heal the impact of attachment insecurities on your romantic relationship.

My hope is that this book will help you and your partner develop a connected and more *secure* romantic relationship.

CHAPTER 1

How Attachment Insecurities Develop

As an infant, you didn't get to choose your parents. Instead, you got handed the parents you were dealt. Your primary caregivers probably did the best they could based on their own lived experiences. For many parents—especially first-time parents—there is typically a learning curve when it comes to understanding and responding to their child's needs. Most primary caregivers foster a more *secure attachment* as they learn to balance structure, support, and love while allowing their child to build healthy connections and interdependence in their life. However, if you were raised by more *insecurely attached* caregivers, you had a higher chance of developing attachment insecurities. These can include trust issues, misinterpreting others' intentions, or a tendency to lash out or shut down during conflict, which may be patterns experienced within your romantic relationship.

Attachment theory research informally began in the 1930s from studying children in hospital settings and foster care environments. In these early studies, it was noted that a lack of physical touch and unstable living conditions caused many of these children to experience a *failure to thrive*. According to Brown and Elliott (2016), a failure to thrive in hospitalized infants was identified in those who were underweight, refused to eat, routinely ignored or emotionally neglected, denied access to seeing their parents due to concerns about spreading infection, and experienced significant developmental delays in both their speech and autonomy.

It should be little wonder that many of these infants sustained chronic infections and had difficulty feeling wanted or cared for in an environment that did not provide necessary emotional support. Conditions that commonly include emotional deprivation, limited physical affection, and a lack of warm and positive interactions between child and caregiver create an environment that limits a child's ability to form a secure attachment. It also places them at a higher risk for developing an insecure attachment style (Brown and Elliott 2016).

Similarly, children who moved around from one foster caregiver to another often failed to develop lasting positive attachments. Due to these children being quickly transferred among foster homes, caregivers were discouraged from emotionally bonding with them (Brown and Elliott 2016). As a result, many foster children experienced little desire to interact with other children or their foster caregivers, lacked emotional expression, and experienced emotional neglect.

In both situations, the children experienced gaps in their emotional development, which affected their ability to connect with others (Bakwin 1942). What was found from these early studies is that *primary caregiver deprivation* negatively impacted the young child's ability to form positive, lasting, and healthy attachments with others. These studies provided a backdrop for what would later become attachment theory.

Human attachment studies formally began with John Bowlby, who expanded on earlier studies in infant attachment in animals (Harlow 1958). In his research, Bowlby (1969) suggested that infants bond with their primary caregivers based on that caregiver's ability to reliably and predictably provide protection while supporting their infant's emotional growth and basic needs. Caregivers who are more in tune with their own feelings and needs are more likely to model healthy behaviors that foster a more secure attachment style for their child, including healthy emotional regulation, interdependence and trust, and a safe environment that allows for individuality (Mortazavizadeh et al. 2022).

If you were provided a secure base in your formative years, you likely became an adult whose early experiences led to higher-quality relationships with those in your life, including your relationship with your romantic partner. However, if your primary caregivers were unable or unwilling to provide you the love and stability you needed as a growing child, your adult relationships may reflect these deficits, along with patterns associated with a more insecure attachment style.

Learning Love Equals Pain

Caregivers (typically the person who identifies as "mom") who are insecurely attached tend to condition their child's attachment style based on what is comfortable and familiar within their own attachment style. For example, if a mom developed attachment insecurities stemming from her own childhood, she may feel uncomfortable offering up affection, encouragement, or emotional support to her child based on what was taught as "normal" in her early development. If the mom's caregivers responded harshly or punitively toward her as a child, she may now respond insensitively or dismissively toward her child's emotional needs. This approach may extend to how she parents her child: whether she provides consistent safety and protection, or whether she displays a lack of compassion and emotional disconnection toward her child. Hence, what she may have been taught as comfortable can be learned by proxy and repeated as familiar.

On the flip side, if a mom grew up with more securely attached caregivers and experienced a relatively stable environment that fostered consistent reassurance for her attachment needs, any emotional distress she experienced was likely reduced by her parents' continued responsiveness. Thus, each time her parents positively responded to her needs for attention, protection, and support, she was likely being taught to continue seeking support, knowing that she would be comforted (Bosmans et al. 2020).

A key consideration when it comes to fostering a secure attachment for a child is recognizing that the parent should be providing consistent affirmation, reassurance, protection, and emotional validation—with the keyword being "consistent." When parental responsiveness is consistently provided, this in turn can condition the child's behavior to continue turning to their parent for their attachment needs being met, knowing the parent will respond. This pattern of seeking out comfort and safety and *consistently* receiving positive support and validation are what help foster a secure attachment style. Contrarily, an insecure attachment style often forms from inconsistent responding or intermittent nonresponses from a caregiver, as will be discussed in much greater detail throughout the book.

It should be noted that while existing research often refers to the maternal caregiver as the primary caregiver, it does not minimize the importance of paternal caregivers in your life. If, growing up, your primary male caregiver had a more secure attachment style, this may have operated as a buffer from having experienced an insecurely attached maternal caregiver. However, if both primary caregivers had an insecure attachment style, or one caregiver was absent in your formative years, these early experiences could influence how your attachment style developed in your childhood or how it evolves throughout your life.

If your caregiver's needs were consistently ignored or minimized in their childhood, they may have become an adult with a more *avoidant attachment style*, which is characterized by a dismissive parenting style, minimal compliments or emotional support, or a lack of consistent comfort and affection. Their attachment style may have been reflected in how they parented you, including patterns of unhealthy responding toward you that may have been chronic, repetitive, and invalidating. This is one way conditioning is established and often reinforced.

For example, if your parents shamed you when showing any vulnerable emotions such as crying, you may have quickly learned that crying equals harsh punishment. As a result, you may have shut off vulnerable emotions and only displayed emotions that were approved by your caregivers. This is an example of *behavioral conditioning*— through the process of reinforcement or punishment, you learned to protect yourself around certain caregivers, or around certain displays of emotion.

On the flip side, if your parent's early experiences were shaped by inconsistent caregivers who provided them intermittent positive attention mixed with intrusiveness or dismissiveness, your caregiver may have developed a more *anxious attachment style*, which again may have shown up in how they parented you. These parenting patterns can include inconsistencies with responding to your needs; they are distant one moment or overbearing the next. For example, on one hand your parent may have been intrusive or overprotective and not allowed you to have any personal space when it came to making friends or spending time alone, leaving you feeling intruded upon. Yet, on the other hand, they may have been neglectful in teaching you how to work through disagreements with your friends, making you feel alone and further distressed.

The reality is that as a young child, you probably wanted a chance to bond with your caregivers, and you may have jumped through hoops to prove your worth, settled for crumbs of external validation, or turned a blind eye to your parent's inconsistent behavior or cruelty. These can impact the quality of your self-worth and your ability to develop a secure and healthy connection with others in your life. It is these types of emotionally unhealthy or invalidating environments that can condition you to learn: love equals pain.

Breaking Free from the Anxious-Avoidant Trap

Now that you have learned a little bit about the history of attachment theory, along with some key terms, you are ready to dig a little deeper. In chapter 2, you will find out about three types of attachment insecurities and how each are conditioned, reinforced, and often carried with you from childhood and into your romantic relationship.

CHAPTER 2

The Three P's of Attachment Insecurity

Not everyone who grows up in an invalidating environment will develop attachment insecurities. Because of individual differences, some situations you may have experienced in your childhood may not have caused attachment insecurities, while others may have. There is ample research supporting that while your attachment style tends to remain relatively stable throughout your life, there are skills you can develop that support a more secure attachment style, some of which are included in this book. Thus, your attachment style becomes less important than the tools you use to help yourself feel more secure within your relationships.

It is important to recognize that fostering a deeper understanding and acceptance of your and your partner's unique attachment styles first starts with learning what to look for in each of your typical patterns. Do you shut down during arguments? Does your partner? Does one of you tend to lash out or continue seeking reassurance or closure while the other walks away after an argument? Does one of you need more time to themself when coming home from work? Does one feel nervous if they don't hear from the other throughout the day? These are common patterns seen in an anxious-avoidant trap that, if left unresolved, can lead to relationship unhappiness for one or both partners. Each of you has unique experiences that have helped shape your attachment styles and how you respond within your relationship. These should come to light as you continue reading this book.

It should also be noted that this book is not written to point fingers or blame your caregivers but to offer insights into the complexities of attachment insecurities, their potential impact on your romantic relationships, and how to foster connection with your partner. There are certain early experiences that can affect your ability to securely bond with your primary caregivers during childhood. These experiences are typically reinforced, or strengthened, through conditioning that begins in infancy and often continues into adult life. If your caregivers were securely attached, they probably fostered healthy connection by teaching you how to love from a place of authenticity and vulnerability.

On the flip side, your parents may have taught you what love is by showing you what love is not. I refer to this situation as stemming from the three P's of attachment insecurity: parentification, people-pleasing, and perfectionism. Each of these core attachment insecurities can influence how you feel about yourself, the "role" you may have been handed in your childhood, the type of attachment style developed, and the quality of your romantic relationships.

Parentification

Parentification is identified as a role reversal between caregiver and child whereby the child may be controlling or resentful toward their parent, or may provide their parent with emotional support, encouragement, or guidance that is developmentally inappropriate (Macfie et al. 2005). For example, a young child may feel responsible for

The Three P's of Attachment Insecurity

making their depressed mother feel happy by trying to make her laugh, showing her funny videos, or trying to get her out of bed. However, over time, the child may start growing angry or resentful of their mother because of her inability to feel happier or to overcome her depression. This may lead to the child scolding or verbally abusing their mother for being depressed and an inconvenience in their life.

There is often an established pattern of conflict, fear, and appeasing behavior with the primary caregiver and patterns of approach and avoidance with the child. This pattern can teach a child to both fear and resent their caregiver, while still reaching out to them for love and support. Many who grow up in these conditions experience both frightening and frightened behavior from their primary caregiver. A common theme with being a parentified child is growing up with an unpredictable caregiver who may be aggressive or have verbal outbursts one minute, while appearing childlike or scared the next. A role reversal between parent and child places the duties of caring for the family on the child's shoulders because the parent may be unsure how to care for themself or their children (Main 2000; Main 1990; Main and Hesse 1990).

When there is a flip-flop of roles, there are usually underlying conditions in the home environment such that a primary caregiver cannot provide consistency or safety for the child. Therefore, a young child becomes conditioned to take on a role, to play a part, or to perform in order to parent their caregiver or provide comfort and stability in the family.

For example, a parent who is struggling with substance abuse may not be able to get out of bed, so the responsibility may fall on the child to handle their parent's hygiene or to ensure that bills are being paid on time. This can lead to feelings of contempt and resentment in the child for having to care for their parent, with little care or compassion being offered to them. Equally common is a mismatch in roles, which often extends from one generation to the next. What you may have been taught in childhood as normal was likely carried over by your caregivers from their childhoods (Macfie et al. 2005).

If you experienced a chronic role reversal in your childhood, you may have become an adult who has learned that the only way you can feel safe or of value is by tossing out your own basic needs to feel wanted or loved, and continuing to care for others, often leading to a pattern of *enmeshment*. Minuchin (1974) coined the term "enmeshment" as a way of describing how families or couples may become overly involved in each other's lives and where boundary violations, such as a lack of autonomy or personal space, are common. Enmeshment is often the result of adverse experiences, addiction, or mental health issues within a family. In enmeshment, a person's boundaries and individual space are minimized, and over-concern for others within the family reduces each person's independence.

This is also a form of behavioral conditioning: if receiving validation or attention in childhood was contingent on you caring for those who should have been providing safety and warmth for you, what is being learned is:

Self-abandonment = intermittent reinforcement in the form of external validation

Let's break down this equation further.

Self-abandonment is a pattern of neglecting your own emotional and physical needs in order to "keep the peace" with others. This may include ignoring your own mental or emotional health for the sake of dodging confrontation with someone. For example, you may have experienced a traumatic breakup, but instead of allowing yourself to process the pain and loss, you may have buried yourself in work, a new relationship, or helping out a family member. When you are in the habit of self-abandonment, many times it is reinforced and maintained by feelings of unworthiness and shame, which can leave you feeling vulnerable, resentful, or emotionally drained. This can become a never-ending loop of continuing to self-abandon in order to avoid confrontation, self-reflection, or upsetting others.

Intermittent reinforcement is a pattern of behavior that is supported or acknowledged every now and then, or only some of the time. This can place you at an increased risk of continuing to please and appease a person in hopes that this time your efforts will be praised or recognized. Using the example above, the child may try to make their mother smile by showing her several funny videos, telling her some jokes, or getting her outside for a walk. Yet, the child does not know which video, what joke, or how long of a walk it may take to make their mom feel better and receive validation from her.

External validation consists of the validating messages we receive from others that make us feel "good enough" about ourselves or our actions. These include praise and attention. Put together, they can strengthen a pattern of continuing to abandon yourself as you care for others, in order to feel valued or to avoid introspection. This pattern has negative consequences on the development of a healthy sense of self-identity and self-worth, and can breed dependency or codependency. In other words, it may lead to a sense of not knowing who you are outside of feeling an obligation to care for others.

In addition to experiencing self-abandonment, a role reversal in your childhood can also affect your ability to express your thoughts, feelings, and emotions in a healthy way, therefore impacting the quality of your romantic relationships. You may struggle to regulate your emotions because of constant stress experienced in childhood, which may have left you vulnerable to overreactivity, or heightened sensitivity. There may now be a pattern of pulling toward a partner to receive the validation and comfort you need, or shutting down out of fear of being rejected or abandoned.

Experiences of parentification often leave a person vulnerable to abusive romantic relationships that reinforce the role you adopted in caring for others. An abusive relationship typically includes choices in partners who have histories of destructive and narcissistic behavior, and who commonly struggle with their own mental health or addictions, leaving you at risk for continuing a caregiver role. Abusive and trauma-bonded relationships are characterized by intense highs and lows, severe enmeshment, loss of identity, coercive control, and cycles of abuse and manipulation, followed by intermittent calm. A key pattern seen in severely toxic relationships includes the makeup-to-breakup dynamic that walks hand in hand with the intense emotional highs and lows.

Toxic relationships overlap with narcissistic and abusive relationships wherein one or both partners have emotionally intense or controlling behaviors. These traits include an inflated sense of entitlement and self-importance, lack of empathy, high levels of manipulation and gaslighting, emotional instability, and intense fears of abandonment. You may have experienced several narcissistic romantic relationships where each time you engaged with a new partner there was hope that they would offer you the consistency you didn't receive in your childhood or in a previous relationship. Instead, you may have found yourself in a pattern of self-abandonment again and again, while letting unhealed attachment insecurities continue to replay. Because trauma-bonded relationships are not the focal point of this book, we will revisit this topic only briefly in chapter 8.

With regard to an anxious-avoidant trap, patterns of early parentification are much less toxic, but they can take an emotional toll on a partner nevertheless. For example, an anxiously attached partner may feel it is their responsibility to be an emotional cheerleader for their avoidant partner by trying to soothe them or offer encouragement each time they shut down after a bad day. Similarly, an anxious partner may be handed the task of maintaining emotional connection with their partner while trying to have a difficult conversation about finances or intimacy.

Parentification Self-Checklist

Below is a self-checklist to gauge where you may score with parentification. Use a pen and paper to write down which of these parentification behaviors or patterns you feel you may have learned growing up. Also included are common signs of parentification seen in romantic relationships.

- ☐ You experienced profound and chronic neglect or abuse in childhood.

- ☐ There was a substance abuse disorder or other addictions in the home.

- ☐ One primary caregiver was not present due to death, divorce, being emotionally disconnected, being a "deadbeat" parent, or similar.

- ☐ You grew up in poverty or regularly lacked essential basic needs such as food, warmth, electricity, comfort, or safety.

- ☐ You moved around often; there was limited stability or consistency.

- ☐ A primary caregiver had a serious medical or mental health condition.

- ☐ You dropped out of school or had to work while attending school to support your family.

- ☐ You or your siblings had roles that you participated in each day, such as cleaning or cooking.

- ☐ You identified as the peacemaker in the family.

- ☐ Your emotional needs went unmet or were met with rage, aggressive outbursts, or shame.

The Anxious-Avoidant Trap

- ☐ You felt deep guilt or shame for taking time to yourself or your needs.

- ☐ You provided emotional, financial, or psychological support to your caregiver (they may have played a victim as a form of manipulation and care-seeking).

- ☐ In romantic relationships, you feel the need to put your partner's needs before your own.

- ☐ You tend to attract (or be attracted to) partners who have severe mental health challenges, be abusive, or struggle with addiction.

- ☐ You may oscillate between expressions of emotional numbness or emotional volatility.

- ☐ You experience intense bouts of anxiety and depression.

- ☐ You often struggle to maintain boundaries for yourself and your partner.

- ☐ You experience high levels of enmeshment, including increased risk for abusive relationships.

- ☐ Your self-esteem hinges on constantly trying to care for your partner.

- ☐ You struggle with expressing vulnerable emotions (often living in anger) as learned for survival.

Scoring Scale

Count up the number of statements that ring true for you. If your score is moderate or high, all hope is not lost! This book is designed to offer you structured tools, guidance, and options for how to increase communication and intimacy with your partner. A higher score simply suggests certain areas for growth within your relationship. What is important is not so much the score but patterns you may now be starting to recognize.

Low: 0 to 4

Moderate: 5 to 8

High: 9+

People-Pleasing

Core attachment insecurities are typically conditioned early in life, of which, people-pleasing behavior is no exception. Caregivers who are overly needy, inconsistently responsive, and misattuned to their child's needs often condition their child to remain dependent, clingy, or reliant on them for reassurance (Brown and Elliott 2016). For example, children who develop people-pleasing tendencies may be trying to watch for how their parent behaves based on a given situation and respond accordingly. In essence, the child learns what behaviors or emotions to display that will get their parent's attention or provide them approval or validation from their caregiver.

At the core of people-pleasing behavior in a child is a parent who is inconsistent in their own behavior. Parents who are inconsistent in their attention and caregiving may scold their child one day for bothering them when they are trying to cook dinner or pay a bill, and then happily engage with the child the next day for the same behavior. This can create anxiety in a child who doesn't know if what they do (or don't do) from day to day will be what offers them comfort or scolding.

Similarly, many caregivers who are unresponsive and underinvolved with their child's positive emotional development are also overresponsive and overinvolved in their negative emotional development, such as when the child becomes sad, angry, or frightened. This can teach the child to seek out situations that trigger negative emotions to get their caregiver's attention. Ultimately, this leads to the child being conditioned to act out because this behavior receives their caregiver's negative attention (Brown and Elliott 2016).

When boundaries are often crossed, dismissed, or only intermittently reinforced, this can also impact a tendency for people-pleasing behavior in a child. When a parent's anxieties surrounding boundaries and parenting surface, they tend to become more anxious about establishing or enforcing boundaries, which becomes a vicious cycle. This in turn can inadvertently reinforce the child's boundary crossing and subsequent attempts at trying to make amends to please their caregiver.

For example, a parent may be inconsistent in teaching their child to knock before entering their room, so the child may not understand the implications about boundaries and personal space. If the child barges in one day to their parent's room to show them a picture they drew and is not scolded, but then is harshly scolded the next day for barging in without a picture they drew, the child may not be learning about personal boundaries as much as they may be learning to have a picture ready to show their parent when overstepping a boundary (in this case, barging into their room without knocking).

When a parent is inconsistent in their own boundaries, they may be inadvertently teaching the child what they do not want. Thus, because of the parent's inconsistent behavior, what the child is learning by proxy is that inconsistency is seen as normal, which can create anxiety in the child in finding ways to please their parent. Equally common is that many with histories of people-pleasing also have histories of rejection or unpredictability as normal everyday experiences. People-pleasing can become a conditioned response whereby a child may be hyperfocused on their caregiver's mood or learn how to read the environment—either in an effort to feel safe and minimize a pattern of chaos in the home.

If you are in a pattern of people-pleasing behavior as an adult, you may have created a false narrative about your early experiences or romantic relationships to soften the effects of feeling unappreciated or resentful in your efforts to please others. It is not uncommon to have grown up with an overly needy caregiver who was unable to teach you full autonomy because of their own insecurities and fears. Your caregiver may have reinforced your dependence on them or may have been self-absorbed with their own feelings and needs, and pushed yours aside. As a result, you may have learned to constantly scan your environment for the first perceived sign of abandonment or rejection.

In romantic relationships, people-pleasing tendencies tend to walk hand in hand with trying too hard to please your partner, with an overemphasis on proving your value and worth. These conditions are ripe for breeding codependency based on too much togetherness, which also has the side effect of limiting your ability to know and understand yourself outside of your role in relationships.

People-Pleasing Self-Checklist

Below, you will find a quick self-checklist of patterns seen in people-pleasers. Use a pen and paper to jot down which of these people-pleasing behaviors or patterns resonate with you in your childhood and romantic relationships. This checklist is not a diagnostic tool, but it can be used to help guide you in becoming more self-aware on patterns that may be replaying in your relationships.

The Anxious-Avoidant Trap

☐ As a child, you had difficulty saying no to others out of fear of disappointing them.

☐ You constantly needed to prove yourself or your worth.

☐ You often experienced emotional or physical abandonment by a caregiver or parent

☐ Your parents or caregivers were highly inconsistent and misattuned to your emotional needs.

☐ You learned certain "approved" emotions that got your caregiver's attention.

☐ Inconsistent or nonexistent boundaries were "normal" when growing up.

☐ You took on the emotions or experiences of your parent or caregiver, and now your partner.

☐ You can be manipulative; pleasing others is used to tap into your own need for validation.

☐ You experience high levels of resentment or contempt if you feel that your help goes unnoticed or unappreciated.

☐ You tend to overstep boundaries, for example, helping others who have not asked for help or support.

☐ You have been taken advantage of by narcissistic friends, family, or partners.

☐ You experience high levels of anxiety and codependency.

☐ You are not happy unless your partner is happy.

☐ You have difficulty understanding your likes, dislikes, needs, and wants outside of a relationship.

The Three P's of Attachment Insecurity

☐ You feel paranoid or anxious if you believe someone is angry with you.

☐ You are prone to toxic positivity or doing what you can to regain feeling "good enough."

☐ You have a fear of expressing your needs or feelings to your partner.

☐ You have deep fears of rejection or abandonment in romantic relationships that can come across as clingy, needy, or pushy behavior.

☐ You show a pattern of overapologizing, oversharing, or overexplaining.

☐ You have a tendency to be overly responsive or overly reactive toward others, which can come across as demanding, obsessive, or compulsive.

Scoring Scale

If you have a moderate or high score, you are at an increased risk of displaying people-pleasing behavior in your relationships, including your romantic relationship. However, please do not focus as much on the score but rather on the individual checks you made. Each checkmark is simply an area in your early relationships or current romantic relationship that is asking for your attention in helping you become more empowered.

Low: 0 to 4

Moderate: 5 to 8

High: 9+

Now, let's move on to the final P of the three P's: perfectionism.

Perfectionism

A need for perfection is usually learned in childhood from invalidating environments that created unrealistic expectations or hoops that you believed you needed to jump through in order to feel loved or accepted. Many who were raised in these situations experienced narcissistic caregivers who valued image, accomplishments, achievements, and performance over their child's emotional growth. If a child is being praised to perform, the underlying message that child is also learning is to jump through hoops to receive validation or approval of their value.

Perfectionism is not innate; a person is not born wanting to be perfect. Rather, a drive for perfection is often the result of learning:

If → Then

The message being conditioned is—*if* you achieve or accomplish based on your caregiver's expectations of perfection, *then* you are seen as "good enough." If you grew up experiencing this dynamic, you may have had parents who were cruel and demeaning, refused your attempts for love or comfort, or made attention or comfort contingent on making them look good or feel proud. If your caregivers valued perfection, you may have been conditioned to learn dichotomous beliefs about yourself—that you are *either* exceptional at everything you do *or* you must be a failure.

Authoritarian parenting—or parenting that is based on punishment, high expectations, and unrealistic and excessive demands—is at the root of perfectionism. There are two common types of authoritarian caregivers: those who are perfectionists themselves and those who are overcompensating for their own human imperfection by trying to live vicariously through their child's achievements. Authoritarian parenting is based on excessively high expectations,

The Three P's of Attachment Insecurity

either spoken or unspoken, high demands, obedience, competitiveness, and excessive discipline. If these traits were modeled by your caregivers, then you may have been taught to imitate them (Carmo et al. 2021; Lozano et al. 2019). You may have additionally felt unseen and without a voice. Families where perfectionism is valued (or required) are emotionally disconnected, achievement driven, and unempathetic to each other's emotional needs.

If your caregivers did not provide you a safe space that fostered emotional connection and positive attention, you may have learned to disconnect from what you are feeling or may struggle with appreciating the emotions of others. This often manifests as feeling uncomfortable, embarrassed, or angry around others who display similar vulnerable emotions that you may have been shamed for in childhood.

Equally common is to push aside all emotions, especially vulnerable ones such as love, trust, fear, or sadness. And then turn to distractions, which can include anything from pulling fifty-hour workweeks to spending endless hours at the gym to using drugs or alcohol to self-numb. These distractions limit how much emotion is felt, including when, where, with whom, and in what context they are felt. All of these can be reinforcing to feeling emotionally disconnected and numb.

Similarly, you may have a history of keeping your romantic relationships at arm's distance or your emotional investment to a minimum. You may prefer casual sex over risking emotional intimacy that is expected with romantic relationships. If you have a history of superficial romantic relationships, there are usually two things that influence this pattern: 1) by keeping relationships shallow, there is less of a risk of feeling emotionally trapped or engulfed; and 2) superficial relationships lessen the risk of feeling vulnerable or imperfect.

If you have been conditioned to set perfectionistic ideals for yourself, you may turn to distractions for a momentary gain in feeling good enough, followed by another round of emptiness or emotional numbness (Doron et al. 2009). You may notice the same ebb and flow in your relationships, whereby the initial rush of newness quickly fades, followed by feelings of indifference or questioning your investment in the relationship.

Perfectionism Self-Checklist

Now, take a moment to complete the self-checklist below. Use a pen and paper to write down with which of the following perfectionism behaviors or patterns you resonate.

- ☐ You were taught to perform, achieve, or accomplish in childhood,

- ☐ You only received positive attention from caregivers when you were achieving or making them look good.

- ☐ You were harshly punished or shamed for human imperfection in childhood, for example, getting a C on your report card.

- ☐ You were insulted, demeaned, or shamed if you gained weight, had a blemish, or other flaw.

- ☐ Your caregiver compared you to your friends or classmates.

- ☐ Your caregivers placed excessive demands or expectations on you, or made you jump through hoops to prove your value.

The Three P's of Attachment Insecurity

☐ You are an overachiever in your academic endeavors and career.

☐ You have a nagging feeling of never being satisfied with your accomplishments or achievements.

☐ You compare yourself to others at your job or personal life.

☐ You have a low tolerance for human error in yourself and others.

☐ You feel embarrassed or ashamed of others if they display human imperfection (for example, you feel disgusted by a partner who never went to college or works at a menial job).

☐ You may be highly defensive or project your insecurities onto others.

☐ You are prone to addictive behaviors as a way of avoiding intimacy or relationships (for example, workaholism, excessively working out, multitasking, and so forth).

☐ You have high levels of control in your romantic relationships (for example, planning out every detail, expecting compliance).

☐ You minimize or dismiss your partner's feelings as too threatening (for example, using toxic positivity to numb over vulnerable emotions and maintain perfect happiness).

☐ You overanalyze things your partner or others said or did.

The Anxious-Avoidant Trap

☐ You have all-or-nothing thoughts about yourself or your partner that may lead to devaluation.

☐ You confuse relationship conflict as relationship failure on your part (or theirs).

☐ You tend to abandon relationships when emotional vulnerability is on the line.

☐ You expect that you and your partner have the same hobbies and shared interests, or the relationship is boring.

Scoring Scale

Now, count up your total score.

Low: 0 to 4

Moderate: 5 to 8

High: 9+

The self-checklists you just completed are not diagnostic tools, but they can offer you important insights into your personal growth and in helping you to better understand yourself and your partner. You may now be starting to feel more confident in recognizing how attachment insecurities may be showing up in your relationship and becoming more aware of certain patterns. In the exercises that follow, you will be given a chance to flex the insights gained from this chapter.

PRACTICE EXERCISE

Read through the sample vignettes and mark your answer. The correct answers are provided at the end of the exercise so you can check your responses.

Johnny is a twenty-five-year-old man with a history of never feeling good enough, which began in his narcissistic upbringing. He has several exes who refused to show interest in him when he showed up for a date. Or they insulted his choice of clothes if he dressed casually. Johnny notices that he constantly puts his partner first by trying to make him happy, and Johnny often ends up feeling resentful if his efforts aren't acknowledged. While Johnny's partners have had highly successful careers and offered him great advice about his, Johnny has never felt like he stacks up to their unrealistic expectations. He now feels anxious when he doesn't receive positive feedback from his current partner on his career accomplishments.

Johnny seems to have a pattern of dating partners who are:

☐ People-pleasers

☐ Perfectionists

☐ Parentified adults

Answer

Johnny seems to have a pattern of dating partners who are perfectionists. It could also be suggested that Johnny is a people-pleaser, with his attempts at putting his partner's preferences or expectations first and by becoming anxious and fearing rejection when compliments or validation are not forthcoming. This is a common romantic pairing seen in an anxious-avoidant trap.

The Anxious-Avoidant Trap

Sally grew up in a very toxic home environment with two younger siblings. Her mother was diagnosed with several mental health disorders, as well as an addiction to pain medication. She sometimes struggled getting out of bed to take care of her children. Sally's father abandoned the family for another woman when she was young. Since then, her mother's mental health consistently declined.

Sally learned at a young age to cook dinner and clean the house for her mother and siblings when she got home from school. She also routinely comforted her mother, who hadn't moved past her husband's abandonment. Sally struggles with intense anger and resentment toward her mother; Sally feels that she was not allowed her own space.

Now, as a grown woman, Sally seems to attract "broken wings"—partners who have mental health issues, are highly narcissistic, have problems retaining employment, and battle substance abuse.

Sally is likely suffering from the effects of:

☐ Perfectionism

☐ People-Pleasing

☐ Parentification

Answer

Sally is likely suffering from the effects of childhood parentification. It could also be implied that a compulsion to repeat, or *repetition compulsion,* may be in play with her choices of romantic partners. She seems to subconsciously seek out partners who have similar disorders as her mother, which reinforces a pattern of parentification in caring for them. She also seems to mimic her unresolved attachment wounding by creating a cycle of similar experiences within relationships that consistently retriggers her attachment insecurities.

Breaking Free from the Anxious-Avoidant Trap

There are many ways childhood insecurities are taught, conditioned, and carried with you into your romantic relationships. You learned about the three P's—parentification, people-pleasing, and perfectionism—that many living with an anxious or avoidant attachment style may recognize within themselves. Next, in chapter 3, you will explore attachment patterns and how they may be related to your attachment style in your romantic relationship.

CHAPTER 3

What's Your Attachment Style?

Your attachment style can influence your behavior, as well as how you feel about yourself and the quality of the relationship you have with your partner. Therefore, it is important that you do regular check-ins with yourself to not only gauge your own feelings and emotions but to make sure the feelings and emotions you are experiencing are *yours* and not a byproduct of your relationship.

To gain a richer sense of self-awareness and insight into your attachment style and specific patterns, you are invited to complete a few more checklists. The patterns listed offer a more global and *general* pattern of responding that includes family, friends, colleagues, and romantic partners. Be as accurate as you can, as this will provide you more insight into how your attachment style may influence your sense of security and happiness within your romantic relationships.

Because no two people are exactly alike, some may express less anxious or avoidant patterns than others. Or they may only become more anxious or avoidant in certain situations, such as if feeling emotionally vulnerable. As you explore the following self-checklists, you will notice that an *anxious attachment* style is associated with more *hyperactivating* behavior patterns, whereas an *avoidant attachment* style is associated with more *deactivating* behavior patterns. It is these two opposing ways of expressing feelings, needs, thoughts, and fears that influence the quality of your relationships, including the relationship you have with your partner (Cassidy and Kobak 1988; Main 1990).

Before you explore the following checklists, there are a few suggestions to consider:

- It is recommended that you complete these checklists alone to minimize any distractions—such as your partner sitting next to you as you take it or being tempted to do other things that require your attention—that may skew your results. It is important to be as open and honest with yourself as you can be; this will help with a more authentic interpretation of your answers.

- It is not required that both you and your partner complete the checklists, but it's strongly recommended. Doing so can be a helpful launching point in unpacking each of your relationship needs. Some couples choose to complete the checklists individually, and then sit together to go over their results. This can provide clues into patterns that replay in your relationship, the types of arguments you and your partner may have on repeat, and what each of you needs based on your unique attachment styles.

- If your partner refuses to complete the checklists, all hope is not lost. While this could be a sign that they may be more avoidantly attached, this in and of itself is not an indicator of your relationship being in jeopardy. By recognizing your own attachment style and romantic relationship history, you can gain insight into the type of partner you usually attract and are attracted to, which can be invaluable in helping build a more secure attachment in your relationships.

Anxious Attachment Style

People with an anxious attachment style tend to be highly sensitive to rejection or abandonment, and often require ongoing reassurance from their partner as well as a need to be in close proximity to them. Using a pen and sheet of paper, tally how many traits or behaviors you display from an anxious attachment style.

- ☐ Prone to obsessing about family, friends, work, romantic relationships, or self-concept

- ☐ Hypersensitivity to rejection cues from family, friends, boss, partner, and so forth

- ☐ Deep and unmet need to feel good enough

- ☐ People-pleasing behavior

- ☐ Significant trust issues

- ☐ Had a caretaking role in childhood

- ☐ Deep fear of abandonment; may have experienced abandonment early in life

- ☐ Emotional dependency

- ☐ A struggle to understand yourself outside of a caretaking role

- ☐ Prone to codependency in relationships with family, friends, coworkers, or romantic partners

The Anxious-Avoidant Trap

☐ Prone to manipulation to feel valued, seen, and heard

☐ Prone to ruminating on disagreements or difficulty moving on from an argument

☐ Feeling shame for having needs (emotional, safety, belongingness, esteem, physical)

☐ Constant need for reassurance from others in your life

☐ Prone to feeling high levels of resentment or contempt if you feel unappreciated

☐ A history of narcissistic people in your life or those with substance abuse issues

☐ High levels of insecurity; may question your skills, abilities, or strengths

☐ Feeling as though your partner is not emotionally invested in you or your relationship

☐ Difficulty setting and maintaining healthy boundaries

☐ Difficulty being alone or without a romantic relationship in your life

☐ A pattern of starting an argument if feeling unseen or unheard by those in your life

☐ Prone to feeling that your emotions are more complex or deeper than others

☐ Finding your value and worth by trying to fix or rescue others

☐ Harsh reactions to feeling threatened or judged

Avoidant Attachment Style

Now, let's explore patterns seen in a more avoidant attachment style. People with an avoidant attachment style tend to be highly independent and have difficulty with identifying and expressing their emotions. Many also have challenges with emotional closeness and intimacy in their relationships. Use a pen and sheet of paper to tally how many traits or behaviors you display from this style.

- ☐ Prone to high self-reliance, such as little need for friends, family, or significant other

- ☐ Significant trust issues with those in your life; looking for angles or agendas

- ☐ Emotionally disconnected; difficulty labeling emotions; feeling numb or empty

- ☐ Difficulty feeling emotionally vulnerable around others, including partner, friends, or family

- ☐ Avoiding emotional intimacy with others; keeping people at arm's distance

- ☐ Pseudo-independence; wanting to feel close to others but struggling to tolerate it

- ☐ Struggle relating to and accepting the needs and feelings of others

- ☐ Prone to minimizing and downplaying personal issues; difficulty letting others offer support

- ☐ Preferring to be alone than out with large groups of people; tending to distance yourself

- ☐ Deep fear of enmeshment; experienced an intrusive caregiver early in life

The Anxious-Avoidant Trap

- ☐ Displaying narcissistic behavior

- ☐ Highly secretive; you can be rigid with your privacy

- ☐ Poor communication skills that can come off as mean, abrupt, or callous

- ☐ Difficulty providing emotional support when others (friends, family, partner) need it

- ☐ Prone to ruminating on the "ex who got away" or idealizing a past relationship

- ☐ Preferring causal relationships over committed or monogamous relationships

- ☐ Often feeling bored in the monotony of a relationship after the newness wears off

- ☐ Prone to smoothing things over (that is, employing toxic positivity) to minimize conflict or issues

- ☐ Prone to distracted behavior; using workaholism or "busy-aholism" as avoidance strategies

- ☐ Poor responsiveness to other people's emotions

- ☐ Prone to perfectionism

- ☐ Prone to lashing out or shutting down around others' displays of emotional vulnerability

- ☐ Low tolerance for conflict; prone to shutting down or walking out

- ☐ Displaying passive-aggressive behavior

You should now have a clearer idea of how core attachment insecurities in your childhood may have placed you at an increased risk of

40

carrying these insecurities into your adult life, including in your romantic relationship. These wounds can become the foundation for how you learn to respond in general to your relationship based on what was conditioned in your childhood.

Now, recall the three P's of attachment insecurity from chapter 2. Take a moment to notice how many behaviors within the two above self-checklists are aligned with the three P's. This can help shed light on where your core insecurities are and how they may be influencing your relationships.

Scoring

The more items you checked within one of the attachment types above, the greater the probability that those behaviors are representative of your attachment style within most relationships in your life. Typically speaking, most everyone will have at least one or two anxious or avoidant responses, even if they are more securely attached.

My Attachment Style Is _____, Now What?

Hopefully, you now have a better idea of where you and your partner score along the attachment continuum based on patterns you marked. The more boxes checked for each attachment style, the more patterns associated with either anxious or avoidant tendencies. However, having more insight and understanding of where you and your partner each fall along the attachment continuum in *general* is not always enough to provide:

- How your attachment insecurities may be reinforced within your relationship

- How the quality of your intimate relationships are influenced by your attachment style

- Why you may keep attracting the same type of relationship

- How attachment can be more fluid and fluctuate based on your and your partner's styles

How you scored yourself on the self-checklist are simply labels on your lived experiences and your overall attachment system. Your attachment style is not necessarily fixed and rigid; it's more dynamic. While *how* you attach to others throughout your life tends to remain rather stable, the quality of your relationships can influence whether any patterns or feelings surface based on attachment insecurities or relationship stressors separate from your attachment style (Brown and Elliott 2016; Mukilincer 2007).

If you scored as more *avoidantly* attached on the checklist but have found yourself dating mostly anxiously attached partners, the dynamics that replay within a specific relationship may make you feel more *anxious*. You may start to predict how the current relationship will play out based on previous patterns. Or, a worst-case scenario is that you may create a self-fulfilling prophecy of falling into old behaviors that actually reinforce the risk of becoming more anxious around your partner.

If you have a history of dating partners who are demanding or insist on spending all your free time together, this limits your and your partner's ability to retain a level of autonomy in your relationship. It can also breed codependency and make you feel more ambivalent about your relationship. It can lead to you feeling more hypervigilant in looking for things that played out in the past.

For example, Dan, forty-one years old, identifies as more avoidant in his attachment style. He values his time alone to focus on his career as a corporate consultant that has him frequently traveling. He and Sofia have been dating for about a year and a half. For the past three months since they moved in together, Sofia has become more demanding of his time, especially when he is traveling for work. She routinely calls him, texts him, and becomes panicked when he cannot answer her calls or texts when she wants him to.

Initially, Dan started sending her a text that he was in a meeting and would call when he got out. However, he quickly began noticing that this seemed to trigger her into sending more texts and then trying to call him, so Dan ultimately started shutting off his phone before meetings. Dan notices he has started feeling anxious when traveling because he knows it's just a matter of time before Sofia begins calling and texting him with her demands and questions.

In this situation, Dan has become more ambivalent in whether or not he wants to continue his relationship with Sofia. He has started to dread her calls or texts because she has become more demanding about knowing his whereabouts and accusing him of cheating on her. He admittedly feels anxious at his job, feels drained in the relationship, and does not know how to fix this issue.

This dynamic is very common in an anxious-avoidant trap and can be exhausting to navigate without support. However, as you will soon read, learning to apply tools such as perspective-taking and building empathy can go a long way in learning to respond with intention to your partner's needs, while still allowing space for your boundaries.

Now, let's assume you scored as more *anxiously* attached and have a history of getting involved with more avoidant partners who are more analytical and emotionally disconnected. This dynamic can make you struggle in trusting your own feelings and emotions based on your partner's inability to remain emotionally present in the relationship. Just as a more avoidantly attached partner (like Dan) is at risk for feeling more anxious depending on the relationship dynamics that keep replaying, a more anxiously attached partner can also begin feeling more avoidant or withdrawn. You may begin pushing away, limiting conversations, responding with hostility toward your partner, or behaving in other ways that are uncharacteristic to your attachment style. These actions can reinforce (strengthen) the push-pull within your relationship.

For example, Janae, thirty-two years old, is more anxiously attached. She has a history of fast-tracking romantic relationships, admittedly feels scared and nervous when not in a romantic relationship, and seems to fall hook, line, and sinker for avoidantly attached partners who ultimately end up hurting her. Her beliefs about romantic relationships are that she wants her partner to be her best friend, her soulmate, and someone she can always count on.

Janae admits that in the past her philosophy on love hasn't always worked out for her. She's had avoidant partners who often became mean or hostile, or stormed out of the relationship, leaving her deeply heartbroken. But, she is hopeful that Steve, twenty-nine, is The One. Janae has been trying to be patient with him when he pushes away from wanting to talk or shuts down when she tries to emotionally connect with him. However, recently she has started to shut down when he does, and she has become more distant toward him. She is scared that something is wrong with her and questions if she really loves him anymore.

In this situation, Janae has begun to take on more avoidant patterns and has started shutting down when Steve does. She has become more withdrawn toward Steve and questions her feelings about him. However, as you will soon read, this may not necessarily be a bad thing. Pausing, reflecting, and taking time to absorb your romantic relationship dynamics may create a sense of feeling disconnected, a sense of urgency, uncertainty about what to feel, or uncertainty about what to do next. Yet, how you handle the uncertainty can be critical in recognizing both your and your partner's relationship needs. By applying the tools in this book, you can begin to navigate through any feelings of uncertainty and eventually strengthen the bond between you and your partner.

Now, let's take a moment to practice what we just learned about anxious or avoidant attachment styles.

PRACTICE EXERCISE

The purpose of the following practice exercises is to gain more insight into your and your partner's unique attachment styles based on the checklists you just completed. Now, grab a pen and your journal or a sheet of paper and complete the following prompts.

1. Based on how you scored on the checklists, write your attachment style findings in your journal or on your sheet of paper.

2. If your partner completed the checklists, write down what you notice about their attachment style.

3. Explore the list of anxious patterns and avoidant patterns from the self-checklists. Which ones resonate with you? Which ones do you feel resonate with your partner? Why?

4. Next, write down three things you would like to address and explore within your relationship. Where do you believe these patterns started? Did they play out in other relationships you have had with other romantic partners, coworkers, family, or friends? What themes emerge?

Breaking Free from the Anxious-Avoidant Trap

In this chapter, you've gained insight into two opposing attachment styles—anxious and avoidant—and the common behavior patterns and traits associated with each. You are on your way to becoming more comfortable recognizing patterns within your own attachment style, as well as becoming more familiar with your partner's style. Next, in chapter 4, we will dive into patterns commonly seen in an anxious-avoidant trap, including common signs and how to move past them.

CHAPTER 4

Insecurities in the Anxious-Avoidant Trap

One of the biggest aha moments for you may be in learning to recognize your unique attachment style. This operates twofold. First, by becoming more aware of some of your own patterns that replay within your romantic relationship, you gain self-awareness into your attachment insecurities, your unmet needs, and how your early experiences may be overshadowing the way you approach your current relationship. These newfound insights into your own patterns are not always going to be easy to accept.

Second, by recognizing your own patterns, you can also get a snapshot into your partner's unique attachment style and the similarities (yes, *similarities*, which you will read about later in this chapter) that may be establishing—or reinforcing—the patterns between the two of you. However, I believe it is important to first examine the differences commonly seen and experienced between anxious and avoidant attachment styles before we explore their shared similarities. Whether your partner chooses to reach a place of insight and awareness for their part in maintaining an unhealthy dynamic in your relationship is something they will need to do. Remember, it is not your responsibility to resolve their part in your relationship issues.

It is natural to feel confused, scared, or even unsure if you want to continue your romantic relationship with your partner. After all, if you and your partner aren't seeing eye to eye on the little nuances surrounding your relationship, does that mean you should throw in the towel and assume you won't ever see eye to eye on what really matters? The short answer: no.

Existing research provides clues into how opposing attachment styles operate, such as how patterned behavior between anxious and avoidant partners may show up in a relationship. Yet, even if you are aware of both your and your partner's attachment styles, and have made peace with how different you both are, it can still leave more questions unanswered with regard to whether these core differences can effectively be addressed and healed.

For example, several studies in recent years have unpacked unique patterns of responding between anxiously attached and avoidantly attached partners with regard to a perceived threat, such as jealousy or intimacy issues, within the stability of a romantic relationship. What makes these findings so interesting is how each attachment style responded, by either trying to "get inside their partner's head" in order to more accurately assess what they believed their partner was experiencing, or by trying to "stay out of their partner's head" due to the risk of destabilizing the relationship (Rholes and Simpson 2004; Rholes et al. 2007; Simpson et al. 2011).

Anxiously attached partners responded more often with ways to help them get inside their partner's head to better understand what their partner may have been thinking or feeling, even if it meant compromising the stability of the relationship. Avoidantly attached partners responded more often with ways that helped them stay out of their partner's head, even if it meant avoiding relationship stressors and hurting their partner's feelings. In other words, each partner seemed to respond based on how their attachment system would presumably react, given a situation that may have been triggering or destabilizing to their relationship.

The takeaway is that anxiously attached partners will commonly react by pulling closer and seeking answers, whereas an avoidantly attached partner will tend to react by pushing away and seeking distance. Thus, the study's findings reinforced perceived differences between the two attachment styles.

However, while these studies show differences in responding based on anxious or avoidant attachment styles when facing a relationship threat, they can also strengthen these attachment differences. In essence, it becomes a circular argument that maintains how "different" these opposing attachment styles are. Instead, it is my hope that after reading this book, you will have a fresh perspective on what makes these differences in responding less polarizing. Both you and your partner can explore your relationship from a clean slate—and with an appreciation that you both may actually be more similar than different.

Hyperactivated Attachment System

There is ample research suggesting that if you are an anxiously attached partner, you typically approach relationships from a sense of desperation to be chosen. It is this desperation that guides your behavior in wanting instant contact with your partner. It also leads you to becoming fearful and scared if you believe that your partner is not responding within a timeframe you expect or in a way that soothes your anxieties. When validation and approval from your partner are forthcoming, it alleviates your fears and provides you a sense of feeling seen and heard. If validation is not forthcoming, it triggers your insecurities.

For example, if you text your partner a little thinking-of-you text and do not hear back within a few hours, you may go right to final jeopardy with self-defeating thoughts, and your actions may follow suit. Instead of looking at the situation as your partner being at work, possibly in a meeting, maybe on the road and unable to respond, or with a phone on silent mode, you might jump to irrational beliefs that they are cheating on you or that their nonresponse is their way of trying to tell you that they do not want to be with you. In other words, you may internalize their delayed response as something being wrong with you—which there is not. Once your attachment system is *hyperactivated*—that is, fears of rejection or abandonment have been triggered—it does not matter what reasons your partner may give you for not answering their phone, because the damage is done and your wound is triggered:

- If they say they were in a meeting → You may question with whom and start comparing yourself to other people who you find better than yourself.

- If they say they were busy preparing for a deadline → You may question what deadline and why they didn't tell you about it.

- If they come home late from work → You may wonder whom they were with and start ruminating on other times they came home late as validation of your fears.

It is these irrational beliefs that reinforce your feelings of insecurity within the relationship and are at the root of feeling misunderstood, judged, or even unloved by your partner. It is also these insecurities that can cause trust issues within your relationship and form doubts that overshadow an ability to form a healthy and secure connection with your partner.

These patterns of trying to establish, or reestablish, closeness to calm fears of being seen as not good enough for your partner are commonly referred to as *hyperactivating strategies* and include the following behaviors (Brown and Elliott 2016; Levine and Heller 2010):

- Thinking only about your partner, difficulty concentrating on other things

- Remembering only their good qualities

- Putting them on a pedestal; underestimating your talents and abilities while overestimating theirs

- Attempting to have constant contact with them throughout the day, such as via text, phone calls, and so forth

- Believing this is your only chance for love

- Believing that even though you are unhappy, you had better not let go

Deactivated Attachment System

On the flip side, if you are more avoidantly attached, there is also ample research suggesting that you may typically retreat from relationships out of a desperation to retain your sense of autonomy. It is this desperation that guides your behavior by pumping the brakes when things get too emotionally intense. You may have a pattern of shutting down when faced with ultimatums or questions about the future of your relationship. Or, you may push away if you feel trapped by your partner wanting more of your attention or time than you are comfortable giving.

For example, if you are an avoidantly attached partner, you have likely learned to rely on yourself and to keep things to yourself. You may not feel a burning desire to tell your (anxiously attached) partner every nuance or detail that happens throughout your day while you are at work. You may keep texts or communication short, to the point, and void of emotional fluff. You may not say "I love you" to your partner within calls or texts. You may consider mundane work meetings as boring or driving an hour to meet a client as annoying and not worthy of casual chitchat with your partner.

So, you may leave these things ambiguous while keeping the conversation to the bare-bones minimum. Instead of looking at the situation as an opportunity to invite conversation and emotional connection with your partner, you may look at bringing these things up to them as validation of why you would rather not talk about them. Yet, it is these patterns that shut down opportunities for building connection with your partner and can be triggering to an anxiously attached person. Once your attachment system is *deactivated* (that is, your attachment insecurity and fears associated with intimacy and closeness have been triggered), it does not matter what your partner says or does. Everything becomes overwhelming and is used as validation to shut down, push away, or retreat back into your personal space:

- If they want to know how your day is going → You may limit what you say to them as a way of redirecting the conversation, in order to expend less emotional energy.

- If they tell you they love you → You may immediately feel overwhelmed or somehow responsible for their feelings if you do not say it back.

- If they want to know about planning that summer vacation together → You may dodge their questions or leave things ambiguous by telling them you will get back to them.

It is these dismissive actions that typically maintain your feelings of insecurity within the relationship and are at the root of feeling overwhelmed, misunderstood, or even unloved by your partner. It is also these insecurities that may keep you feeling emotionally unsafe, which can further trigger your need to run and push away.

These patterns are commonly referred to as *deactivating strategies* and can include the following behaviors (Brown and Elliott 2016; Levine and Heller 2010):

- Saying or thinking, "I am not ready to commit," but staying together nonetheless

- Focusing on small imperfections in your partner (for example, how they talk, dress, or eat) and allowing them to get in the way of your romantic feelings

- Pining after an ex-partner

- Flirting with others

- Not saying "I love you" or otherwise implying you do not have feelings toward the other person

- Pulling away when things are going well

- Forming relationships with an impossible future

- Checking out mentally when your partner is talking to you

- Keeping secrets and leaving things foggy

- Avoiding physical closeness

Are you starting to now see the hyperactivating or deactivating strategies that you use? Or that your partner uses? Now, let's turn your attention to the exercises below to test yourself.

PRACTICE EXERCISE

Hopefully, you are now more familiar with the common activating and deactivating strategies used by someone with an anxious or avoidant attachment style when feeling overwhelmed or emotionally vulnerable.

1. Please take out a sheet of paper and a pencil or use an electronic journal to draft two columns.

2. In the first column, write your partner's name. In the second, write your name.

3. Jot down two or three ways you commonly react toward your partner when feeling your attachment system activated or deactivated.

4. Begin exploring similarities in how each of you reacts using an **If → Then** format. For example, *if* you typically react a certain way to your partner coming home late from work, *then* what is their typical reaction to it? Or, *if* they send you multiple texts trying to get your response while you are at work, *then* how do you typically react?

5. Write down what are you starting to notice about these patterned ways of reacting between you both. What can you start doing to make healthy changes to your patterned reactions?

Avoidant Attachment vs. Narcissistic Behavior

I want to take a moment to shed light on several traits that commonly pin an avoidantly attached person as being a "narcissist." First, simply because a person has a more avoidant attachment style does not in and of itself make them a narcissist. Second, "avoidant" is an attachment style, whereas "narcissism" is associated with a personality disorder. The two are not synonymous. Narcissistic personality disorder is something that is only diagnosed by professionals and should not be self-diagnosed. All too often, the word "narcissist" is causally tossed around on social media or among social circles, when in reality it is a clinical disorder that should not be used to label someone who is simply vain or selfish.

Some descriptions can blur the distinction between avoidant attachment and narcissistic behavior. For example, infidelity, ignoring or dismissing future plans, or looking at a person's imperfections as reasons to devalue them can be popularly viewed as synonymous with avoidant attachment. But the reality is that these tend to hinge more on narcissistic behavior. An abundance of academic literature correlates narcissistic traits of entitlement, lack of empathy, a need for constant admiration, and a dislike for being alone as associated with narcissism and the behaviors described above (Campbell and Miller 2011; Kernberg 1985). Of course, these are not always associated with a narcissistic personality, as anyone may be inclined to engage in this behavior.

It's perhaps more important to look for what may be motivating a person's behavior and their tendency to push away. For example, looking for imperfections in a person may be a sign of many things, including narcissism and avoidant attachment. Yet, what is driving their behavior? Are they hyperfixating on their partner's physical imperfections as a reason to discard the person? This may suggest narcissistic traits associated with image, status, or vanity. Or, are they looking at their partner's imperfections as a way of pushing away any romantic (vulnerable) feelings they have about the person and as a way of trying to reestablish their autonomy? In this situation, a more avoidantly attached person may fixate on imperfections, such as how their partner acts when angry. Or, they may become annoyed with their partner's need for open communication, which may be seen as overwhelming and threatening to their sense of independence.

Similarly, "future faking" is commonly associated with narcissism at the idealization ("love bombing") phase of the relationship. Yet, this may be confused with fears of making future plans out of a worry of becoming emotionally vulnerable, which is typically associated with avoidant attachment. Hence, as with anything, it is important to explore what may be motivating a person's behavior before jumping to conclusions that they must be a narcissist.

Triggering Each Other's Wounds

As discussed earlier, most existing research on attachment styles (and most couples living with differing attachment needs) tend to hyperfocus on the obvious differences that can continue driving a wedge between you and your partner. Here is a list of common patterns experienced within an anxious-avoidant trap. The goal of exploring this list is not to notice any "differences" between yourself and your partner but to examine how each of you may be engaging in these types of behaviors and reinforcing the patterns.

Some common patterns include:

- One partner may struggle being alone if they are not in a romantic relationship.

- One partner may prioritize their career over their partner.

- One partner may get clingy if the other person does not provide them enough reassurance that the relationship is stable.

- One partner may struggle with expressing their emotions.

- One partner may become more demanding of the other person's time if they are not home when they said they would be.

- One partner may routinely shut down when discussing issues about finances or splurging.

- One partner may feel misunderstood and judged for wanting more of the other person's time.

- One partner may fail to let their partner know where they are going or when they will return.

- One partner may want or expect to spend all of their free time together.

These patterns are very common in an anxious-avoidant dynamic. What you may need or want with your partner is often on the other side of the relationship coin from what they seem to need or want from you. It is this dichotomy that can create a rift between you and your partner, and the push-pull phenomenon we've been discussing. Ultimately, what you may have initially found endearing about your partner at the beginning of your relationship can become the thing you start resenting about them as your relationship progresses, leaving one or both of you wanting to throw in the towel.

For example, Abby, a thirty-eight-year-old marketing executive, has spent most of her adult life marching to the beat of her own drum. She is proud of her fierce independence, has spent the last seventeen years of her life building her career, and does not feel she needs to report to her partner, Shana. Abby feels Shana is treating her more like a child than a partner when Shana asks Abby to check in with her when she's out with friends. On the other hand, Shana, who is a thirty-nine-year-old orthopedic surgeon, expresses that Abby rarely makes any attempts to communicate her whereabouts when she's out with friends. Abby says she only wants to ensure that Shana's safe, given that she tends to drink when reconnecting with old friends.

Both Abby and Shana have valid points:

- Shana sounds as if she is emotionally invested in the relationship and is concerned about her partner's whereabouts, given that Abby drinks when with friends.

- Abby sounds like a very independent and self-sufficient woman who has not had to answer to anyone before and is struggling with "checking in" with Shana.

Who's right? Who's wrong? Let's explore.

Common Insecurities in an Anxious-Avoidant Trap

There are three common insecurities experienced between partners in an anxious-avoidant trap: *fear of intimacy, communication issues, and feeling misunderstood.* As you read about these relationship challenges, see if you can unpack which attachment insecurities may be influencing Abby and Shana's relationship and their unique behaviors. Most important, see if you can find solutions on how they can navigate these wounds and reach a deeper connection.

Fear of Intimacy

A fear of intimacy shows up differently in relationships depending on a person's attachment style, lived experiences, learned patterns, and any unprocessed attachment disturbances. Intimacy is not limited to physical intimacy; it also includes emotional intimacy within a romantic relationship. Simply put, intimacy is any behavior, verbal or nonverbal, that creates an opportunity for connection and bonding between two people.

For example, in his book *The Five Love Languages: The Secret to Love That Lasts*, Gary Chapman (2010) discusses five expressions of love that are common within romantic relationships: acts of service, quality time, words of affirmation, receiving gifts, and physical touch. These love languages can be simplified into what you identify with as an act of love you prefer receiving from your partner. Figuring out what type of love language resonates with you helps in fostering intimacy and connection between you and your significant other. However, there are many more nuances surrounding intimacy and perceived fears, as you will soon read.

A fear of intimacy is actually two sides of the same coin. On one side, a fear of intimacy can emerge as a fear of abandonment; on the other side, it can show up through distancing behaviors or as a fear of closeness, also called *engulfment* (Brown and Elliot 2016). While the outward behaviors guiding a fear of abandonment or engulfment tend to look like polar opposites, the driving motivation for both boils down to a fear of *intimacy*. If you fear being abandoned, any closeness to others can trigger this fear. You may find yourself fixating on your partner's every word, reading between the lines, and looking for the first sign that they are going to leave you. This can lead to you desperately trying to get closer to them.

On the flip side, if you fear being engulfed, any closeness to others can trigger a sense of feeling consumed, overwhelmed, or trapped within the relationship—as if you are losing parts of yourself. You may notice that you tend to avoid situations that require your full attention or emotional energy. You may become hypervigilant around people who you feel are expecting more from you than you are comfortable giving, and you can find yourself desperately trying to get away from them.

As with most maladaptive patterns, a fear of intimacy typically starts in your formative years. It is often the result of unpredictable, unreliable, and inconsistent caregivers or invaliding environments. If you are more anxiously attached, these fears tend to surround hypervigilance with any perceived threat of rejection. For example, you may notice that you dissect every word or behavior your partner says or does, while looking for the first sign of disapproval (Mukilincer et al. 2003). It is these unhealthy fears that limit your ability to connect with your partner from a healthy space. Each time your attachment system is activated, your fears of being abandoned move front and center. Once activated, it can be difficult to redirect your thoughts and energy to something less threatening.

This activation also triggers an increased risk of engaging in behaviors associated with *separation distress* (Bowlby 1969). Within romantic relationships, separation distress is often referred to as protest behavior, whereby a more anxiously attached partner may engage in behaviors such as testing their partner's emotional investment, seeking constant reassurance, or displaying jealous or accusatory behavior when their fears surface (Levine and Heller 2010). The irony is that while these protest behaviors are done to try to get your partner's attention, they are counterproductive to intimacy and may increase the potential for being rejected or abandoned.

If you are more avoidantly attached, your fears of intimacy often include behaviors aligned with pseudo-independence or avoidance of anything perceived as emotionally threatening to your sense of independence. You may notice you lack a fear of being abandoned and tend to avoid or minimize physical or emotional closeness (Collins and Reed 1990; Wei et al. 2005). You may value your sense of independence over a romantic relationship. You may believe that relationships often feel exhausting and overwhelming. You can easily distract yourself with other things that provide less emotional investment.

It is common to overlook what your partner may be feeling by shutting down your own emotions. It is these distancing behaviors that affect your ability to connect with your partner in an authentic and vulnerable way. Once you feel emotionally vulnerable and threatened, your attachment system deactivates. This deactivation actually reinforces tension and protesting from your anxious partner. The irony is that by using deactivating strategies to reduce feeling overwhelmed in the moment, you are actually increasing the potential for continuing to feel engulfed in your relationship. In other words, each time you shut down or turn away from your partner, you trigger their fears and re-create a situation that is counterproductive to allowing the distance and space you want.

Signs of Fear of Intimacy

Fears of intimacy can be common in many romantic relationships, especially if one or both partners are more insecurely attached.

However, these fears are often at center stage within an anxious-avoidant trap because of opposing attachment styles and individual needs. Which ones do you see happening within your relationship?

- Clinginess or a need to be close to your partner (anxious attachment)

- Pushing away or a need for personal space from the relationship (avoidant attachment)

- Loose and inconsistent personal boundaries (anxious attachment)

- Tight and overly rigid personal boundaries (avoidant attachment)

- Need for constant reassurance (anxious attachment)

- Need for autonomy (avoidant attachment)

- Projecting your insecurities about yourself onto your partner (anxious attachment)

- Projecting your insecurities about the relationship onto your partner (avoidant attachment)

Moving Past Fear of Intimacy

To move past fear of intimacy, you must first recognize whether you are fearing abandonment or fearing engulfment. These steps include:

1. **Don't pin your fears on your partner.** Chances are, your fears have been longstanding and started in your childhood, often from an invalidating or negligent environment.

2. **Differentiate.** Explore whether you tend to fear abandonment or engulfment more often. Notice when these fears are triggered. What happened just before you felt this core wound surface?

3. **Have the tough talks with your partner.** This is perhaps even more important as your relationship progresses, in order to build a more solid foundation. It is okay to speak your truth, let your partner understand where you are coming from, and tell them what your unique needs are.

4. **Learn tools.** Find ways that help you systematically recognize and build your own sense of safety and emotional security, while learning to recognize where your partner is in their sense of safety and security (see chapter 5).

5. **Find emotional balance.** Learn to balance emotional self-reliance with emotional interdependence within your relationship. All-or-nothing thinking and behavior have no place in a healthy and committed partnership.

You have just been introduced to distinct ways that both anxiously attached and avoidantly attached partners may react when feeling emotionally vulnerable, including how fears of intimacy can show up within your relationship. Keep these points in mind as you complete the following exercises.

PRACTICE EXERCISE

Now, take a moment to review the list of common signs of fear of intimacy based on either anxious or avoidant attachment. Then, answer the questions below. You may want to take out a sheet of paper and pen to jot down your response.

1. Do you notice that you are more anxiously attached or avoid-antly attached?

2. What attachment style do you feel your partner has?

3. When it comes to clinginess or pushing away, which do you resort to more often? Which does your partner resort to? Dive deeper and explore where clinginess or pushing away may have started and what core wound may be driving this behavior.

4. Now, repeat step 3 for boundaries and reassurance versus autonomy.

Communication Issues

Healthy communication is one of the biggest predictors of a satisfying and emotionally connected romantic relationship. By engaging in healthy communication, you can openly express your needs. It fosters being curious, engaged, and interested in what each other says without judgment. When communication is healthy and collaborative, there is an equal level of appropriate turn taking, pausing, reflecting, waiting for the other person to understand and respond, and listening and speaking.

An ability to engage in healthy communication is also a sign of a more secure attachment between partners. It's marked by a high level of meaningful engagement that includes emotional displays appropriate for the context. Not surprising, many communication failures are common in insecurely attached relationships, with perhaps the most frustrating breakdowns in communication happening between one anxiously attached partner and one avoidantly attached partner.

If you are more anxiously attached, communication *excesses* tend to happen. This includes talking too fast, veering off topic, speaking for someone, not allowing the other person to get a word in edgewise, speaking too loudly, demanding too much effort from the listener to remain engaged, and being overly dramatic, especially when angry or when fears of abandonment are triggered (Brown and Elliott 2016).

If you have developed a more anxious attachment style, you likely experienced inconsistent caregivers. These caregivers may have vacillated between being neglectful and seemingly uninterested in what you had to say one moment to being overly intrusive or demanding the next. Because of these types of early invalidating experiences, you may have become more hypersensitive to perceived rejection. This may have left you feeling insecure or overwhelmed in trying to get your point across. The reality is, the more reactive your speech, the less responsive your partner may become—which is counterintuitive to what you want: connection and communication with them.

If you are more avoidantly attached, communication *deficits* tend to happen. This includes not speaking up when you should, not talking at all, shrugging a conversation, using overly positive references (toxic positivity) to downplay vulnerable emotions, and intellectualizing. You may toss out facts instead of feelings or may use a dismissive or invalidating tone to minimize your partner's feelings. If you are angered, you may resort to shutting down or walking out when resolution is not offered. Or, you may become fixated on your point and refuse to see the other person's perspective (Brown and Elliott 2016).

If you have developed a more avoidant attachment style, you likely experienced caregivers who were unresponsive to your emotional needs. They may have been harshly punitive, punishing, or shaming for any expressions of emotional vulnerability. Because of these early types of invalidating experiences, you may be less in tune with your own emotions. You may struggle expressing what you want to say out of fearing being seen as "wrong." However, the reality is that the less responsive you are with understanding and relating to both your and your partner's feelings and needs, the more reactive they may become in trying to get you to meet theirs. This is counterintuitive to what you want: to feel safe in your relationship with your partner, while still allowing time to yourself.

Signs of Communication Issues

Communication issues are very common in an anxious-avoidant trap because of each partner's opposing needs. For example, more anxiously attached partners often require specific and thorough communication in order to help them feel more secure within their relationship. This is perhaps most important during times of conflict. However, more avoidant partners may not provide validation or may leave things vague due to their resistance with vulnerable displays of emotion. Which challenges to communication are seen in your relationship?

- Answering for your partner (anxious attachment)

- Dodging any answer or giving a very vague response (avoidant attachment)

- Assuming you know how your partner feels or speaking for them (anxious attachment)

- Being unsure of how you feel and leaving emotion out of most conversation (avoidant attachment)

- Talking too loudly or too fast (anxious attachment)

- Talking too softly or too slow (avoidant attachment)

- Interrupting often during conversation (anxious attachment)

- Not taking the initiative to start a conversation (avoidant attachment)

- High levels of ruminating on a single topic (anxious attachment)

- Avoiding vulnerable topics or redirecting conversation to a more neutral one (avoidant attachment)

- Demanding, controlling, and complaining speech when angry (anxious attachment)

- Defiant refusal to see the other person's perspective or feelings when angered (avoidant attachment)

Moving Past Communication Issues

To move past issues with developing and maintaining healthy communication with your partner, you first need to recognize your communication style and then your partner's. Consider these actions:

1. **Soften your approach.** It can help to first write down or text yourself what you want to say. Start with a compliment that you appreciate about your partner or your relationship. These "soft starts" are less confrontational and open the door for both partners to feel seen, heard, and understood (Gottman 2015). Then state the issue at hand.

2. **Take responsibility for your actions.** Take responsibility for how you have been reinforcing possible ruptures in communication between you and your partner, but don't take responsibility for their role.

3. **Avoid pointing fingers.** Don't play the blame-game. Instead, use "I" statements and try to include your feelings. Be sure to avoid assuming you know how your partner feels or what they are thinking. Instead, ask.

4. **Become an active listener.** Practice learning active listening skills (see chapter 8, "Building Intimacy in Your Relationship") that allow you both to speak freely, without the risk of being interrupted or shutting down.

5. **Pay attention.** Check in regularly with each other. Watch for body language (such as fidgeting, crossed arms, or not looking at each other). Pay attention to whether you or your partner need a break or time to process things.

PRACTICE EXERCISE

Breakdowns in communication are some of the most common issues in romantic relationships, and they're especially common in an anxious-avoidant trap. The following exercise will encourage you to notice communication breakdowns with your partner. You'll be invited to explore whether you are more anxiously attached or avoidantly attached. Grab your journal or a sheet of paper and take a few minutes to respond to each of the writing prompts in sequence.

1. Describe one recent situation between you and your partner where there was a breakdown in communication. What was the problem? How did you react? How did your partner react?

2. Next, reexamine the problem from a deeper understanding of how you both may be more similar than different. Explore the idea that a communication breakdown is really a need for a deeper understanding of each other's perspectives and needs.

3. Next, take a moment to go over the list of "Signs of Communication Issues" and explore whether you tilt toward more anxiously responding or avoidantly responding.

4. Do you notice that your partner responds differently? If so, how?

5. Now, mentally explore what you can do when a communication rupture occurs. Consider the following questions: What is the topic that caused the rupture? Is it the same topic that has caused one before? How have you previously responded during this breakdown in communication? How have they responded?

In action, this is how an anxiously attached partner may respond to the previous step:

The argument is about wanting more of their time and physical touch. Each time I feel vulnerable or need to be reminded that I am loved, I approach my partner and reach in for a hug. They either freeze or barely give me any physical contact. I feel like they retreat by ignoring me.

I notice this is the same pattern that replays each time I feel unseen and unheard and want them to hold me, and I become angry and accuse them of not loving me.

I can now try to:

- *Become (and remain) more self-aware of my communication style toward them, along with my behavior.*

- *Become (and remain) more self-aware of their communication style toward me without feeling demanding or insistent.*

- *Learn to validate myself if they are unresponsive in the moment, while letting them know how I appreciate their closeness.*

- *Change my perspective on how they show me love and affection by writing down five things they do to show their emotional investment.*

- *I can explore if I am overlooking their efforts or placing demands on how I expect them to show me love.*

Insecurities in the Anxious-Avoidant Trap

If you are more avoidantly attached, this is how you might respond to the same step:

The argument is about me needing time to myself. My partner expects me to hold them all the time, and I get frustrated with it. I feel that they are clingy or won't let me get anything done on my own. I hold them for a few minutes, but it never feels like it is enough. They say things like I didn't put any effort into holding them, which makes me want to push away more. I feel like I am walking on eggshells waiting for the argument to start.

I can now try to:

- *Be more aware of when they approach me for physical touch as their way of trying to feel loved by me.*

- *Become (and remain) more self-aware of how we speak to each other. I can let them know my needs and feelings more consistently while still meeting theirs.*

- *Teach myself that how my partner expresses their need for love may be different than my needs, and that these differences should not be seen as a problem.*

- *Change my perspective on how they ask me for affection. I can write down five ways to give them affection, including increasing how much emotional vulnerability I show them, while also asking for some personal space afterward, if I need it.*

- *I can explore if I am dismissing their needs by providing a few examples of how I typically shut down or push away.*

Remember, it is equally important that your partner is also on board with learning new, adaptive ways in meeting your needs (and theirs) while retaining both your and their boundaries. If you are doing the work and they aren't, nothing changes.

Now, let's turn to the third challenge commonly seen in anxious-avoidant relationships, feeling misunderstood.

Feeling Misunderstood

Misunderstandings are a part of every relationship. You will likely feel misunderstood or judged at least once in your romantic partnership. A misunderstanding happens when partners are not seeing eye to eye on the issue at hand and may not be getting a clear picture of what the other person is saying or needing. This can lead to making assumptions, jumping to conclusions, or feeling disconnected from your partner. Over time, and if left unhealed, feeling misunderstood may even lead to feelings of contempt toward your partner and your relationship (Gottman 2015).

When you and your partner understand each other, you are recognizing not only the verbal cues of what the person is saying but the nonverbal cues as well. When there is a high level of understanding each other, you can safely assume you each know the other person's feelings, needs, and thoughts about a given situation. With a high level of understanding, there is also a sense of consistency and predictability within your relationship. Neither partner is pulling the rug out from under the other person's feet; each partner recognizes the relationship nuances that identify your unique connection with each other.

These insights into how you and your partner learn to understand each other are based on past experiences together. Ideally, you have both learned to recognize each other on a deep level. Yet, this is not always the case. Many couples will routinely misinterpret their partner's needs or feelings. They may arbitrarily assume something that turns out to be wrong, leaving the other person to feel misunderstood.

If you are more anxiously attached, you likely struggle when things are ambiguous or vague in your relationship. You may opt for offering direct actions and words to your partner as your way of helping them understand your needs. Yet, this may be misunderstood by an avoidantly attached partner as being demanding or bossy. Being highly in tune with your own feelings and your partner's may be misconstrued as being dramatic when it comes to how you engage in relationships, leaving you feeling ashamed for expressing your feelings. You may have a pattern of needing to hear that you are wanted, loved, and appreciated that may come across as overly needy. If you have an anxious attachment style, you may also struggle with low self-esteem and may see your partner as better than yourself; your need to be reminded of your value and worth may be misconstrued as demanding or dependency.

On the flip side, if you are more avoidantly attached, you may commonly feel misunderstood when it comes to emotional intimacy. Keeping intimacy at arm's distance may be misinterpreted as rejecting your partner's love. A fear of losing your autonomy may be internalized by an anxiously attached partner as not wanting them. You may struggle with what you are feeling or how to express it in words, which may be misinterpreted as acting narcissistically toward your partner's feelings. Your need for autonomy and time to yourself may be seen as selfish or as a lack of investment in your relationship. Similarly, you may offer indirect or vague responses to your partner as a way of keeping your autonomy, which may backfire as coming across as rude or condescending. While you want to let your partner in, you may build walls to protect yourself from feeling unsafe, which can be misunderstood as cruelty, entitlement, or superiority.

Signs of Feeling Misunderstood

Feeling misunderstood is something that most, if not all, couples will experience at least once in their relationship. Misunderstandings are based on differences in emotional vulnerability and communication style. However, if you are in an anxious-avoidant trap, these differences can feel overwhelming and be reinforcing to any feelings of stress and tension between you and your partner. Explore the list below to determine which common signs of feeling misunderstood resonate in your relationship:

- Ambiguity from a partner without a clear-cut response (triggers anxious attachment)

- Too many questions or an incessant need from your partner to answer them (triggers avoidant attachment)

- Overthinking or hanging onto every word your partner says (anxious attachment)

- Not putting much effort into what your partner says or feels (avoidant attachment)

- Hypersensitivity to rejection or feeling misunderstood by your partner (anxious attachment)

- Hypersensitivity to feeling trapped and misunderstood by your partner (avoidant attachment)

- Hypervigilance surrounding your partner's feelings about you (anxious attachment)

- Hypervigilance surrounding your feelings about your relationship (avoidant attachment)

- Jumping to the worst-case scenario about your partner's limited emotional expression (anxious attachment)

- Feeling resentful and shutting down with expectations of needing to show more emotion in your relationship (avoidant attachment)

It can be very painful feeling misunderstood in your relationship, especially with someone who is supposed to relate to you and understand you. Next, we will turn to ways to help increase feeling seen and heard.

Moving Past Feeling Misunderstood

To move past feeling misunderstood by your partner, consider these actions:

Don't assume. Ask for clarification. On the flip side, don't let your partner make arbitrary or impulsive conclusions; ensure they are also asking for clarification.

Be Aware. Become self-aware and regularly check in with yourself. Are you feeling tense? Notice your partner's reactions. Are they becoming more dismissive? More anxious? These provide clues on how to respond with more intention and not react on impulse.

Acknowledge differences. Be mindful that you and your partner may have different ways of processing information or may require differing amounts of time to process something (avoid overthinking or dismissiveness).

Take a different perspective. Put yourself in their shoes. If your partner is more avoidantly attached and tells you they want time to themself, take it at face value. Recognize if you are drawing conclusions based on your own attachment insecurities.

PRACTICE EXERCISE

This exercise will allow you to start gaining more insight into where in your relationship you or your partner may feel misunderstood.

1. Please get out a sheet of paper and pen, and take a few minutes to examine one disagreement in each of the challenges discussed in this chapter: intimacy, communication, and feeling misunderstood.

2. As you write, consider the following questions: What caused the challenge? How was it resolved? How can you help prevent this challenge moving forward? How can your partner respond?

Breaking Free from the Anxious-Avoidant Trap

In this chapter, you were introduced to common insecurities seen in both a more hyperactivated (anxious) attachment style, and a more deactivated (avoidant) attachment style. You also explored three common insecurities seen between these two attachments styles, including fears of intimacy, communication issues, and feeling misunderstood, and how these insecurities can manifest for each attachment style. Next, in chapter 5, we will begin a deep dive into safety needs and three of the most critical safety needs we all have.

CHAPTER 5

Exploring Basic Safety Needs

When you think of the word "safe," what comes to mind? If you are like most, you probably envision being in your home, surrounded by loved ones, where there is a sense of security that protects you from intruders or outsiders. You may have a high-end alarm system to complement the deadbolt and security camera at your door. You may have windows with multiple locks or live in a gated community with a hired guard. You may be in the habit of always parking in well-lit areas at the mall or double-checking your appliances to make sure you turned off the coffee pot before leaving for the office.

These are the kinds of things people do to provide themselves a sense of safety in their environment. Yet, at the end of the day, these habits may be of little protection and may only offer a superficial sense of safety. The bottom line is that if someone really wanted to break into your home, even an alarm system may not keep them out. And, even if you double-check to make sure you turned off the coffee maker, it may not be enough to prevent a short-circuited electrical fire.

Feeling safe is one of the most basic and fundamental needs of all humans. When there is a threat to your sense of safety, you may immediately react by attempting to avoid the threat and trying to reestablish a sense of security. If someone drives erratically or dangerously, you swerve to avoid their car. If you hear on the news that there is an impending hurricane, you secure your windows and doors, hoping to minimize any damage. These are ways you may try to strengthen your sense of physical safety in your immediate environment and to minimize feeling unsafe.

I am not suggesting that security cameras, properly locked doors, defensive driving, and preventative measures won't make you feel safe. They will. However, there are other forms of safety that are much deeper and more profound than structural safety. It is these other forms of safety that can help provide clues into how you engage in your relationships, including your common go-to patterns. The reality is that you may be unaware of how an unmet need for safety may have influenced your choice of partner in the past or how you see your relationship now.

So, what exactly is *safety*?

Emotional Safety

It should be a no-brainer that if you feel safe in your relationships, you should also feel a sense of emotional well-being. Feeling secure within your relationship is something that happens organically and over time as you and your partner build trust and a sense of mutual understanding. However, feeling safe is much more nuanced than simply knowing your partner's quirks or their habits. The reality is that many go through their lives not recognizing whether their relationships are promoting an authentic sense of safety or what their unique safety needs are.

Exploring Basic Safety Needs

It can be difficult to navigate your blind spots when it comes to unmet safety needs, especially if these needs have not been recognized as going unmet. First, I want to make a distinction that if you are in an abusive relationship, it is necessary to seek professional support so you can safely leave. Abusive relationships such as trauma bonds are not sustainable and will continue jeopardizing your overall safety. Second, if your relationship is not abusive but you are struggling with an anxious-avoidant trap based on attachment insecurities, then this book can offer you support in helping build a healthier bond with your partner and in feeling more secure.

According to Abraham Maslow and his theory of motivation (1962; 1943; and Fraser 1987), his hierarchy of needs reflect the basic needs of all humans. In his original model, there are five levels of basic needs: physiological, safety, belongingness, esteem, and self-actualization. These needs are outlined in a pyramid format, with the most primal physiological needs at the bottom of the pyramid, followed above by safety needs, belonging needs, and so on. While there is no hard or fast rule for identifying from one level to the next, it is important to recognize where within each level you may have deficiencies in your needs.

Lesser unmet needs can influence your ability to level up within the hierarchy. For example, if you have deficits in one or more basic safety needs, these unmet needs may continue showing up in other areas of your relationship. This can affect your overall well-being. After all, if your need for predictability (a safety need, discussed below) is missing or incomplete from earlier in your life (Maslow 1943), this unmet need can influence your ability to feel wanted, loved, or accepted by your partner. In other words, it can be tough—if not impossible—to ever feel wanted or loved if you are struggling with how to feel completely secure in your relationship.

I believe three of the most important safety needs are *predictability, reliability,* and *consistency,* which will be addressed next. Deficits in

77

these needs can affect your overall sense of security within your relationship, including how attachment insecurities may bleed into areas within your romantic relationship.

Keep a couple things in mind when reading this chapter. First, all insecure attachment styles have unmet basic needs, which may include some unmet safety needs. How these unmet needs show up within your relationship will depend on several factors including: your attachment style, your partner's attachment style, both your and your partner's level of self-awareness, and whether either of you have sought support in the past.

So, begin by exploring how your unmet safety needs may differ from your partner's. For example, you may have unmet safety needs for stability and security in that you require emotional support, especially during a disagreement with your partner. However, if they have an unmet safety need to be allowed space and autonomy to process things (especially during a disagreement), your needs will seem misaligned with theirs and can overshadow how each of you feels security within your relationship.

Second, these perceived differences in how your and your partner's unmet needs may surface can offer clues in recognizing and holding space for them. As you read how unmet safety needs can show up in a relationship, the hope is that it sheds light on the patterns that may be replaying behind the scenes. Third, and perhaps most important, the goal is to discover how attachment insecurities may be triggering to unmet safety needs and how you can help heal them.

Predictability

Predictability is often confused with boring. How many times have you heard that someone is so "boring and predictable" that you can set your watch by them? A hard truth is that some people look at prioritizing predictability within their relationship with the mundane.

Yet, predictable relationships are sustainable relationships. When a person is predictable, their attitudes, beliefs, feelings, needs, and habits are stable. Predictable relationships include both a sense of independence, whereby each partner is tending to their own needs, and a sense of interdependence that helps foster connection and intimacy. With predictability, there is no fear of having the rug pulled out from under you, and there is an overarching sense of continuity from one minute to the next.

However, if you experienced significant attachment disturbances growing up, you likely missed out on having a sense of predictability in your environment. If there is a history of unpredictability in your early years, you may not have known what version of your caregivers you were getting from one day to the next. In these situations, there may have been a lack of predictability in how they responded to your needs, in their expectations of you or others, or in their general behavior. In essence, what is being conditioned is that your environment is predictably unpredictable.

For example, your caregiver may have responded with compassion and support in helping you with your math homework one day, while violently yelling and scolding you the next. You may have grown up in an environment where your caregiver seemed more concerned about their own life and left you caring for your younger siblings. You may have moved around a lot, or there may have been frequent changes to economic stability or caregiver employment. Or, you may have had a caregiver who struggled with mental illness, which left them unable to care for themself or your physical and emotional needs (Main 2000; Main 1990; Main and Hesse 1990). These types of unpredictability in your early years not only affect your overall sense of safety but can later influence your romantic relationships.

The reality is, if you grew up in an environment where you felt as if you had little control over what happened to you or how you were treated, you likely gained feelings of deep insecurity and a sense of helplessness within your relationships. Many who experience these types of early environments become adults who have learned to over-control everything in their lives, leaving them at an increased risk for codependent adult relationships, perfectionistic tendencies, and compulsive patterns as a result of having been parentified (see chapter 1).

Impact on Adult Life

As discussed in chapter 1, the effects of parentification are often extensive and long-standing. These effects can influence whether you feel there is predictability in your life and within your relationships. While many who experienced parentification can find themselves in highly narcissistic and toxic relationships (see chapter 8), this is not always the case. If you were a parentified child, it can have a less severe but equally damaging effect on your relationships and can show up as a compulsion to rescue or caretake those around you. The main reason some engage in this pattern of behavior is because fixing their environment operates as a form of control, offering a momentary sense of predictability.

However, over time, this pattern reinforces victim-rescuer roles whereby one person needs fixing while the other comes in as the rescuer. Equally common is seeing a flip of victim-rescuer roles, whereby you and your partner switch between fixing and needing fixing as an overarching theme in order to maintain a sense of pseudo-predictability within your relationship. This is especially common in codependent and enmeshed relationships where there are other relational deficits, such as struggling to experience authentic connection or vulnerability outside of the dramatic overtones within the victim-rescuer roles.

When there is a tendency to overcompensate in your romantic relationships by needing to rescue those around you, it is usually done to help you feel safe and to provide a sense of predictability in your environment. Hence, learning to notice this pattern in yourself or your partner can help you heal.

Predictability is one of the most important safety needs we have. If our sense of predictability was compromised growing up, it can leave us vulnerable to feeling unsafe in our romantic relationship. Now, complete the next exercise and explore your answers with regard to your romantic relationship.

PRACTICE EXERCISE

First, it is important to recognize that spontaneous and fun are not the same thing as *unpredictable*. When checking to see where you and your partner score on predictability within your relationship, focus on things like stability, speech patterns and inflections, attitudes, how you both react when angry, how you each express vulnerability, and overarching patterns that help identify the traits of the person you fell in love with. In essence, when looking to see how much predictability your relationship offers, consider the day-to-day happenings as a good place to start.

1. Begin this exercise by getting out a pen and sheet of paper, or using a journal. Both you and your partner may want to allow each other to answer the following questions uninterrupted. This can be an excellent way to begin unpacking similarities, differences, and how you each interpret things like feelings and thoughts as they are experienced by the other person. This exercise can also be used as a catalyst in fostering healthier communication.

2. Start with each partner discussing how you both seek out order and stability in your relationship.

3. Does having a sense of order (routine, daily tasks, balance, and respect) seem different for each of you? Or, do you both seek out a sense of relationship order similarly? For example, if there is a disagreement, how do you typically respond? How does your partner typically respond?

4. Do you notice an overarching sense of predictability in how you respond to relationship stressors? In your partner's? Write down five ways that you and your partner seek out predictability within your relationship as a form of safety between you both. What patterns do you notice emerging?

Now it is time to turn to the next important safety need, reliability. As you read, see if you can glean ways that reliability shows up in your relationship.

Reliability

Reliability is similar to predictability in that it can include daily routines or order when it comes to how a person engages in their relationships. However, one distinction to consider is that predictability is based on knowing *how* a person will engage in a certain routine daily activity, feeling, or thought, whereas reliability is based on knowing *whether* they will engage in it.

Reliability must exist for both you and your partner to trust each other, and to provide a safe foundation in your relationship. A main part of reliability is responsibility, meaning that you and your partner each own up to your shortcomings and work together to support the sustainability of your relationship.

However, if you or your partner experienced unreliable caregivers in your childhoods, this can influence your ability to trust others or to count on them to be there for you in your moment of need. For example, if your parent forgot to pick you up from an after-school ballgame one time, it will probably not be too traumatic for you. But, what if they routinely forgot to pick you up after school some days? Or most days? These patterns then become associated with unreliability, which dramatically reduces your ability to trust them and count on them.

Unreliable caregivers are undependable; they are often highly self-absorbed, may have unpredictable tendencies, and may be harshly punitive, especially when obligations are placed upon them, such as the daily demands of parenting. They may impulsively change the subject if you ask for their guidance about something. Hence, you may not know whether they will hold the same feelings, thoughts, or behaviors from one day to the next. Unreliable caregivers may have been intrusive, violating of your personal space, or suffering from their own mental health challenges. They were therefore likely unresponsive to your emotional needs while being overly attuned to their own.

Many who experienced unreliable caregivers develop an anxious or avoidant attachment style because of the parent's inability to attune to their child's physical and emotional needs. For example, if you were reared by caregivers who were neglectful in meeting your needs, you may have learned to rely only on yourself and to view the world and everyone in it as untrustworthy and unreliable. These conditions may create an environment ripe for developing an avoidant attachment style, whereby you learned you must find a way to meet your own emotional and physical needs.

On the flip side, another sign of unreliable caregiving is based on emotional unreliability, whereby a caregiver may be intrusive and demanding of you one day, and loving and easygoing the next. This type of environment can create an anxious attachment whereby you may not know whether your caregiver is going to be supportive or punishing, based on your parent's feelings or needs from one day to the next.

Impact on Adult Life

The effects of growing up in an unreliable environment are significant, especially on your ability to trust yourself and others in your life as reliable. As with most things, the effects of having had an unreliable caregiver in your childhood can affect you along a continuum.

On one end, it may be that you are more easily annoyed or feel irritated over a slight such as your partner coming home from work late for date night plans. You may find yourself trying harder to please and appease your partner or begin keeping a mental tally of other times they came home late. These patterns run the risk of becoming resentful toward your partner or your relationship, especially if you feel unseen or unheard.

Similarly, you may be uncomfortable turning to your partner for validation or emotional support because of fears they are not fully committed to you, leaving you with a sinking feeling that you cannot count on them. If you grew up having had your basic needs for a reliable and consistent environment shot down or only intermittently met, it can leave you feeling vulnerable and that the people in your life must not care about you. This can weigh on your self-esteem.

On the other, more extreme end, having experienced an unreliable caregiver in childhood may have left you with deep emotional wounds. If a person who was supposed to be trustworthy, dependable, and predictable in their treatment of you was chaotic, unreliable, or intrusive, it may have affected your ability to trust yourself when it comes to choosing educational or career goals, supportive and authentic friends, or a healthy partner. You may now struggle to recognize your own value and worth.

If reliability was missing or only intermittently reinforced when you were growing up, it may have left you questioning whether you can rely on anyone or whether they are dependable. Next, you will begin to flex your knowledge on reliability and how you see it shown to you by your partner.

PRACTICE EXERCISE

Building a sense of reliability within yourself and your relationship with your partner is an important and necessary step in cultivating healthier and happier connections in your life.

Exploring Basic Safety Needs

1. To begin this exercise, first revisit chapter 3 and reread about attachment styles.

2. Next, grab your journal or a sheet of paper and a pen and write about whether you feel you are more anxiously attached or avoidantly attached.

3. Next, explore by writing whether you feel you had reliable caregivers who consistently cared for your physical and emotional needs. Notice if you had any gaps in reliability with your caregivers. If so, journal about how an unmet need for reliability may be influencing your feelings, beliefs, or patterns within your romantic relationship. This may show up as a tendency to people-please, shut down and avoid turning to people for support (pseudo-independence), or somewhere in between.

4. Finally, explore how you are now more aware of any similarities of unmet needs for reliability between you and your partner, which may show up as polar opposite behaviors.

Up next, is the topic of consistency, which is another necessary safety need. As you read, consider how you and your partner may provide each other consistency in your relationship.

Consistency

Another safety need that is critical in our overall emotional development and for our ability to feel secure in our adult romantic relationship is consistency. Consistency is based on *why*, meaning that a person should be aware of and able to label their motivations—or the reasons for holding certain feelings, beliefs, or patterned behaviors—as routine and cohesive. For example, if someone holds certain beliefs about living in the city, or has a specific morning routine they have engaged in for years, these thoughts or behaviors should be relatively stable and consistent over time, as well as the reasons the person holds for engaging in them.

However, if you were raised by an inconsistent caregiver, it typically means their thoughts, feelings, and behaviors were disjointed and incongruent from one experience to the next. In a nutshell, they were scattered. You may have heard your parents give you the excuse "because I told you to" as a rationalization for doing what they wanted. Or they may have blamed others as their justification, such as "because your dad says so."

If you were not offered any consistent guidance, support, or teachable moments from your caregiver, and were left to your own devices, you were likely made to feel as if you did not matter. For a highly intuitive and sensitive child, this dynamic can especially be a recipe for disaster. If you grew up feeling unsafe in asking simple "why" questions of your caregiver, it was likely because the answer you received was usually different from one day to the next, along with your caregiver's rationalizations for it. In these situations, if you were highly sensitive, you may have internalized your caregiver's dismissive inconsistencies as a sign that you do not matter. Because many who grew up in these conditions have histories of feeling unseen and unheard, you may become an adult who is guarded, distant, or dismissive around others out of self-preservation.

Unmet safety needs for consistency and reliability have many overlapping traits, including the potential for developing an attachment wound of invalidation. However, because at the root of inconsistency is a caregiver's own scattered thoughts, beliefs, and patterns, I believe that anyone who grew up in this dynamic has a greater chance at developing commitment issues and may struggle with their ability to remain emotionally present and available within their relationships. Simply put, if your caregiver was unable or unwilling to keep their own thoughts, feelings, and patterns consistent, they were likely not teaching you consistency.

Impact on Adult Life

If you grew up feeling inconsistently loved, wanted, or valued in your childhood, you may have carried these wounds with you into your adult life, which may be affecting your relationship with your partner. Inconsistent upbringings can be a source of developing an insecure attachment style, specifically a more avoidant attachment style, where you may run hot and cold with your partner and struggle with intimacy.

For example, you may spend a wonderfully passionate vacation together, only to pump the brakes when the reality check of being back home sets in. On the flip side, you may have developed a more anxious attachment style from having experienced an inconsistent upbringing that made you feel as if your needs did not matter. You may now have an excessive need for reassurance from your partner in validating these unmet needs. In the above example, you may struggle with going back to a normal routine after vacation and still insist on more time with your partner. If this does not happen, you may internalize their behavior as something being "wrong" with you.

When inconsistency is taught as normal in your formative years, it can interfere with your ability to relate to and understand yourself. It may leave you struggling to understand who you *are* and your inherent value within yourself. With regard to your romantic relationship, inconsistency can show up as changing your opinion of your own likes and dislikes; your partner's friends, their job, their car; or the plans you made together in saving for a bigger home. Also, inconsistencies between your thoughts and actions may be a reason you hold these opinions. Underneath the superficial inconsistencies are often feelings of deep confusion on how you feel about the relationship, how you feel about your partner, how your partner feels about you, and how you feel about yourself.

PRACTICE EXERCISE

In this exercise, you will explore the theme of inconsistency. Grab your journal and a pen.

1. Write down any signs you see that may resonate with inconsistencies (for example, deep confusion or fears) about how you feel about your relationship, your partner, your sense of self, or how your partner sees you.

2. Explore how these inconsistencies may have started for you or your partner in your formative years, and how they are emerging in your relationship.

3. Now, choose two or three situations in which you feel there are inconsistencies between you and your partner that have replayed within your relationship.

4. Next, write down how each situation played out. For example, do you notice there is a pattern of you or your partner pumping the brakes on fully committing?

5. Do you see any patterns in this behavior, such as occurring after having spent a very romantic weekend away together? Or you or your partner changing up your feelings or opinions on things to just keep the peace or to avoid a confrontation?

6. Now, revisit the same situations you jotted down as signs of feeling unsafe (inconsistent) in your relationship, only this time explore them from the deeper awareness and knowledge you have gained in understanding how and why inconsistent behavior can be learned and carried with you from childhood. Take note of how these inconsistencies in your or your partner's feelings, thoughts, beliefs, or patterns may have been learned from an inconsistent caregiver.

7. Last, explore how to build consistency in your relationship by setting and maintaining boundaries surrounding areas you feel are inconsistent. For example, if you notice a pattern of running hot then cold following intimacy, be clear and up front with your partner about what you see. Allow space for each of you to respond.

8. After allowing some time to reflect, devise a simple plan to support one another. Include ways you can support each other's needs while respecting your own needs for a predictable, reliable, and consistent relationship.

Breaking Free from the Anxious-Avoidant Trap

At this point, you should have a clearer idea of how unmet safety needs can influence your thoughts, feelings, and behaviors throughout your life—most noticeably within your romantic relationship. Next, in chapter 6, you will learn about three critical belonging and esteem needs and how childhood, abandonment or rejection, or narcissistic parenting can negatively affect these needs.

CHAPTER 6

Unpacking Basic Belonging and Esteem Needs

What do the words "belonging" and "esteem" mean to you? You may feel that to belong means you are part of a larger group and that you can show up as your authentic self around your friends, family, coworkers, community, and your partner. You may feel that belongingness is part of your immediate environment and the day-to-day activities that are included within it. To belong may include a need to be an integral part of a system, whether within your social group or neighborhood. Similarly, you may feel that esteem is an inherent part of how you see yourself or a trait that motivates you to accomplish successes in your life or that promotes your sense of belonging.

Belongingness and esteem may be expressed as broader concepts within your culture or country, or they may be experienced within a more intimate environment that includes only you and your partner. When you feel as if you belong, you feel understood and appreciated, which helps promote healthy self-esteem. These feelings can additionally cultivate a sense of personal safety, whereby the people in your environment and your life are predictable, reliable, and consistent (see chapter 5).

Belongingness and esteem can be fluid concepts; they may change and evolve depending on your immediate circumstances. A sense of belonging and esteem can also include your ability to adapt to any changes within your environment. For example, you or your partner may have been offered a job promotion out of state, and you now find yourself having to adjust to a new home, new coworkers, a new neighborhood, and a new community—all of which can impact self-esteem. When facing a different environment or different circumstances and their potential challenges, a sense of disconnection or feeling out of attunement can result. This can make you feel less than or as if you do not belong. This feeling of disconnection can trigger your unhealed attachment insecurities, including any times in your life when you were made to feel as if you did not fit in or were ostracized.

Similarly, esteem can be expressed as how you see yourself, including the views you hold about your relationships and the world. With higher self-esteem, you likely have an equally high level of self-respect and respect for others in your life. You may view relational challenges as opportunities for your personal growth, and you probably have a positive outlook on life in general.

On the flip side, if you have low self-esteem, you may internalize relational issues as your fault, or you may view obstacles as barricades that continue reinforcing your belief that you are not worthy of happiness or respect.

Emotional Well-being

Let's look at a couple of important points here. First, for emotional well-being, you should have been taught what belongingness and esteem are and how to foster them in your life. You cannot be expected to know something you were not taught. Yet, if you were not taught what it feels like to belong or to think highly of yourself, the resulting developmental gaps can influence your sense of wholeness and your ability to connect with others, including your partner.

If you experienced early mistreatment, these gaps in your emotional development can, and usually do, affect your ability to feel as if you fit in or are wanted. According to Abraham Maslow, belonging and esteem needs come after safety needs on the hierarchy (1962, 1943). If you were stuck trying to survive in an unpredictable, unreliable, or inconsistent environment, your belonging and esteem needs would have played second fiddle until your safety needs became more predictable, reliable, and consistent.

Not knowing where you may have unmet belonging or esteem needs can overshadow unmet safety needs and affect your ability to vulnerably connect with your partner. The end result is that your unmet safety needs may now amplify your other unmet needs, which can then take center stage in other areas of your emotional well-being. This includes how you approach your romantic relationship. Yet, if you were not taught how to recognize whether your needs are going unmet, this can become a pattern of replaying dysfunctional dynamics from one relationship to the next in a vain attempt at getting these needs met.

It is very common to try and get your needs met through a romantic relationship, without knowing exactly what or where your unmet needs are. For example, you may turn to your partner to rescue you from your pain without knowing where your emotional pain is or how it started. Yet, because the hole is internal, no external validation or sense of belongingness that your friends, family, or partner may offer you will ever feel as if it is enough. This leaves you feeling as if you are not enough.

In time, this dynamic can become circular and lead to relationship stress, feelings of resentment toward your partner, or ongoing chaos that never seems to get resolved. This cycle will not stop until you unpack your own core wounds while turning inward to validate yourself, instead of looking outward with the expectation that your partner will do this for you.

As you continue reading through this chapter, recall how any perceived differences in attachment styles or coping styles between you and your partner are more about being two sides of the same coin and less about being on opposite sides of the playing field.

Origins of Unmet Belonging and Esteem Needs

This chapter includes three common origins of unmet belonging and esteem needs—*childhood trauma, prior rejection or abandonment,* and *narcissistic parenting*—that can trigger a sense of disconnection within you. While a sense of feeling that you do not belong is commonly associated with an insecure attachment style, experiencing a lack of belongingness is not limited to only insecurely attached people. Anyone can feel as if they do not belong, which can also influence how you feel about yourself and your level of self-esteem.

Yet, a key difference between more securely attached people versus those with a more insecure attachment style is in how they approach and address feeling that they do not belong. Whereas a more securely attached person may feel confident in finding other people or experiences in which to feel connected, an insecurely attached person may have their insecurities triggered by a negative experience, which can be reinforcing to their sense of not fitting in. Over time, this leaves them more susceptible to feeling ostracized by others in their life, which can also affect their overall esteem.

Because unmet belonging and esteem needs are most often experienced in an anxious or avoidant attachment style, these adverse conditions can be reinforcing to any existing gaps in your emotional development. They can also impact your ability to discern between feeling wanted and feeling unwanted. Keep in mind that these three origins do not form an exhaustive list; they are a snapshot of what existing research suggests as reasons that insecurely attached people often struggle with belonging and esteem needs.

Childhood Trauma

Your earliest experiences should have included social interactions between you and your primary caregivers. Hopefully, you learned that your caregiver's smiling face or gentle touch offered you a sense of safety and connectedness. For example, if you fell down while taking your first steps, you may have been offered comfort and encouraged to try again. As you grew, you were likely taught how to socialize with friends, how to share, how to establish personal boundaries for yourself, and how to manage disappointment in your life as external from your value and worth. By having a secure base in learning how to foster your sense of belonging and esteem, you were being taught how to recognize and express your emotions and needs in a healthy and prosocial way.

As an adult, these earliest experiences should have generalized into a solid self-identity whereby you are confident and comfortable showing up as your authentic self with those in your life. These kinds of experiences are what help to create a foundation in feeling that you are wanted—that you have trusting and loving relationships in your life, and are part of a larger group that values and loves you (Maslow and Fraser 1987; Maslow 1962).

Yet, not everyone experiences a healthy and adaptive childhood. For some, early experiences were riddled with rejection due to being raised by emotionally immature parents or in adverse conditions that affected their immediate environment. If you grew up feeling unsafe or unseen, these wounds do not simply go away when you reach a certain age. If anything, they often become *worse*—often deeper and harder to piece apart. Traumatic events can include anything that happens environmentally, such as divorce, poverty, substance abuse, moving around a lot, a death in the family, social injustice, or caregiver unemployment, all of which can affect healthy development.

However, traumatic experiences can also include attachment trauma, such as rejection, abuse, betrayal, or abandonment from a primary caregiver. Both forms of trauma carry significant risks and lasting negative effects on the quality of your relationships. People who have lived through traumatic events often experience lifelong challenges in establishing and maintaining healthy relationships. They may develop poor coping strategies, recurrent depression or anxiety, or chronic physical health conditions (Cruz et al. 2022).

Signs you may have experienced traumatic events in your life include:

- An unpredictable caregiver whom you feared because of their violent behavior but were reliant on for food, shelter, and warmth

- An invalidating environment where your needs were minimized or seen as unimportant, unnecessary, or wrong

- A lack of consistency in what your parent said or did from day to day

- Substance abuse within the family

- Unemployment

- Polyvictimization (for example, social injustice plus poverty)

- High frequency of relocation (common among military families)

- Emotionally distracted caregivers who made you feel unseen or unheard

- Rejection or abandonment (either emotional or physical) from a primary caregiver, friend, or family member

- Unreliability; you may have been unable to turn to your caregiver for support, love, or safety from one day to the next

- Harsh punishment, including physical abuse

- Emotional abuse

- Emotional or physical neglect

Because traumatic situations affect your overall ability to function, it is also common to see overlaps with how these situations may be affecting your unmet basic needs. For example, any unmet belonging or esteem needs may also be reinforcing unmet safety needs, such as having experienced an unpredictable, unreliable, or inconsistent caregiver or environment. After all, how can you expect to feel wanted, loved, or respected if you are unable to feel safe? If you lacked an emotionally safe caregiver in your life, grew up in a toxic environment, or did not have a solid role model to show you that you are valued and accepted, then how you "attach" to others can be reflected in these deficits and in the type of attachment style you developed.

For example, if you ended up developing an anxious attachment style, you are likely highly susceptible to feeling unworthy of a healthy relationship. You may also be at an increased risk for low self-worth and a tendency for people-pleasing. Anxiously attached adults often feel comfortable in situations that trigger clinginess, because this was likely conditioned as familiar responding. People-pleasing behavior may have been encouraged or taught as love by an inconsistent or selfish caregiver; you learned by proxy that this is love. However, this pattern can be reinforcing to your anxiety and the need to please by making it easy to slip into a people-pleasing role while ignoring deeper issues that may be maintaining this pattern.

On the flip side, if you grew up developing an avoidant attachment style, you may shut down and ignore your emotions, likely because emotions were shamed outside of a few approved ones. It is not uncommon to hear that an avoidantly attached person was only allowed to feel happy or numb around their parents, while vulnerable emotions such as fear, sadness, or even love were shamed.

If you are more avoidantly attached, you may feel easily overwhelmed in intimate relationships, as these can trigger your attachment insecurities, including any emotions that you may not have been allowed to express. Those with histories of emotional wounding were not taught that intimate relationships should be a safe space for expressing vulnerable emotions. You may have felt rejected and shamed for being yourself, or you may have experienced emotional abandonment from your caregiver unless you conformed to what they expected. Many with an avoidant attachment style were harshly punished for expressing vulnerable emotions and have since learned to disconnect from them, often making any attachment insecurities that much more difficult to overcome.

Prior Rejection or Abandonment

If you or your partner experienced prior rejection or abandonment early in your life, this can become a sign of abandonment or rejection replaying in your romantic relationships. Keep in mind that physical abandonment due to divorce can also trigger feeling unwanted or not belonging. It is common for anyone who experienced childhood trauma to have also experienced abandonment or rejection by a primary caregiver.

For example, an abusive parent cannot provide you consistent nurturing or guidance, the absence of which can leave you feeling emotionally abandoned. While your caregiver may have been physically present, they may not have provided you a necessary foundation in feeling safe or a worthy part of the family. If you experienced this, you may have internalized it as something being wrong with you.

However, because traumatic events are nuanced and can generalize into other areas of your life, feeling a sense of disconnection or a lack of belongingness is not specific to environmental trauma. If you experienced a volatile upbringing, chances are you were not shown how to choose emotionally stable friends or to feel comfortable in social settings. As such, feelings of abandonment and rejection may have followed you to school, where you experienced bullying, which can further reinforce feeling abandoned and rejected and impact your overall self-esteem.

If you are anxiously attached, you probably know the deep fears you carry with you regarding rejection and may have experienced this at one or more times in your life. Anxiously attached people often believe that others in their life are inconsistent and will eventually leave or hurt them. For example, you may have seen your caregivers go through a bitter divorce, may have witnessed a parent belittling the people in their life, or may have witnessed them chasing after a relationship to try and prevent their own fears of rejection. These experiences can plant a seed in how you cope with fears of abandonment, as well as what you believe about others in your life as potentially abandoning or rejecting you.

Narcissistic Parenting

Narcissistic parenting can produce a shattering of self, which wrongly teaches you that you are only as good as what you do for others, instead of who you are (Mahoney et al. 2016). This also creates a dichotomy whereby you can lose touch with your own feelings and needs because of being conditioned to believe your value and worth hinge on others' expectations. It is this dynamic that can create a perfect storm in your romantic relationship. If you feel you have no value, you can also feel that you are inherently unworthy of connection, regardless of how much your partner loves you.

Narcissistic caregivers are along a continuum: On one end they can be abusive and punitive; they create restrictive environments and excessive expectations of accomplishing or performing to make them look good. On the other end, they may be caregivers who are negligent and complacent. In more extreme cases, both parents may vie against each other, resulting in you receiving harsh abuse from one parent and complacency from the other. The overarching theme in these situations is that your caregivers are not seeing you for who you are but for who they expect you to be (Kermanian et al. 2021; Mahoney et al. 2016).

You may notice a common theme with early traumatic experiences as catalysts for other negative (often emotionally painful) experiences in your life. This may include experiences of abandonment or rejection, or development of a shattering of self from narcissistic parenting. This shattering of self can extend to symptoms of depression, anxiety, a need to feel perfect in order to be accepted or loved, or experiencing narcissistic behavior in relationships.

If you experienced caregivers who were abusive or only offered you contingent validation, it is natural to feel that you must not be worthy of love or respect from your partner. These misbeliefs in how you see and feel about yourself can extend to expectations on your romantic relationship, including fears that you will be abandoned or further invalidated.

Now let's turn to an exercise to help you unpack three common origins of unmet belonging and esteem needs. As you complete the exercise, focus on what may have influenced your unique attachment style, as well as your partner's.

PRACTICE EXERCISE

This exercise invites you to explore common origins of unmet belonging and esteem needs, which can include childhood traumatic events, prior rejection or abandonment, and narcissistic parenting. When belonging or esteem needs are missing or incomplete, it can negatively impact how secure you feel in your relationship or in your ability to believe that your partner authentically loves you. It can also influence how you feel about yourself and the ways that you typically react when feeling emotionally triggered or having your attachment system activated or deactivated.

Please grab a piece of paper and a pen for this exercise. You may also ask your partner to complete the exercise and then exchange answers with each other after afterward.

1. What do the words "belonging" and "esteem" mean to you? How do you express them? How have you seen them shown to you? How were they introduced to you as a child?

2. Do you feel that the three common origins of unmet belonging and esteem needs have affected your self-worth? Have they affected whether you feel like you fit in or belong? If so, how?

3. Did your caregivers help you establish a sense of connectedness within your family of origin or adoptive family? Were other issues happening that made it hard for you to feel that you were wanted within your home or community (for example, poverty, war, abuse or neglect, divorce, race or ethnicity, or socioeconomic status)?

Suffice it to say, having experienced prior trauma or rejection, or feeling a lack of worth, can influence whether you feel as if you are loved or respected by your partner.

Basic Belonging and Esteem Needs

Now, let's look at three necessary belonging and esteem needs: *validation, love, and respect.* We all share these fundamental, basic needs—as well as their potential negative effects, if they have gone unmet.

Validation

Validation is a necessary belonging need that should have been taught in your childhood from caregivers, teachers, and friends. When you feel a sense of validation, it is an acknowledgment from others that your lived experiences and feelings are seen as worthy and relatable. You are offered a sense of connectedness and empathetic compassion. In essence, validation means that your reality is understood and seen as reasonable and respected, which, in turn, gives you a sense of feeling secure and valued.

On the flip side, *invalidation* is where your reality is denied. It occurs "when a person is made to believe that their needs, feelings, or lived emotional experiences don't matter. In essence, if a person is conditioned to believe that how they perceive their world is unreasonable or insignificant, these messages can later generalize to feelings of insecurity and depression, and an unstable sense of self-identity" (Tanasugarn 2022).

If you or your partner grew up experiencing a profound sense of invalidation, this can affect your ability to trust and regulate your own emotions, or to question whether you carry any inherent value. Invalidating environments are those that include emotionally dysregulated caregivers who are unable to relate to or manage their own emotions, and may have harshly punished you for expressing yours.

If you experienced a narcissistic caregiver, you may have had your emotional responses shamed or stifled, especially if you learned by proxy to react with strong emotions to stress. In this dynamic, each time you were harshly punished for expressing an emotional reaction to something, it may have had the *opposite* effect: your caregivers may have ended up reinforcing your heightened emotional reactions because of their refusal or inability to validate your emotional needs.

For example, being slapped for feeling scared or told to go to your room for feeling sad are reactions that invalidate feeling respected or understood. Instead of your caregivers allowing you to express your fears or sadness, their inability or unwillingness to receive your vulnerable emotions may have become the catalyst for experiencing even stronger emotional reactions out of desperation to feel validated. This is one way emotional dysregulation can begin.

Impact on Adult Life

It is common to hear that someone with an insecure attachment style who did not receive healthy or consistent validation has carried with them deep unmet needs to feel seen and heard. For example, if you are more avoidantly attached, you may refuse any attempts at validation from your partner, especially if the only validation you received earlier in your life was contingent on your performance, achievements, or in making your caregivers look good.

So, you may have learned to associate verbal validation as something to not trust while looking for an agenda. As a result, you may not want compliments from your partner and may instead assume there are conditions tied to it. Similarly, you may be uncomfortable giving validation to your partner because of not having had a healthy role model from which to learn this skill. Invalidating childhood experiences may have caused you to distance yourself in relationships when feeling vulnerable or having to depend on others. As a result, you may now push away out of self-preservation.

Contrarily, those who are more anxiously attached may have only received intermittent validation. For example, if your parents were in a good mood, then attention or validation may have been forthcoming. Yet, if they were in a bad mood, you may have been ignored. With a more anxious attachment style, you may struggle with not receiving validation or verbal affirmation from your partner, due to early experiences when you wrongly learned that your value hinged on pleasing and appeasing. You may now find yourself jumping through hoops for your partner or others in your life, with the expectation that they will shower you with praise, compliments, or appreciation.

These unmet needs to feel valued, loved, or respected can come off as overly needy, which may backfire when it comes to getting the sense of validation you are needing. You may start arguments with your partner as a way of getting their attention (after all, negative attention is still attention). Or, you may feel that you have to put your own needs on hold to reestablish balance in the relationship, resulting in a vicious cycle. You may freely give excessive validation to your partner, while they may ask you to cut back on how much praise you are offering up.

At first glance, this can look like you and your partner are on opposite sides of the playing field. Yet, you both may have experienced similar invalidating environments that have left you feeling unseen or unheard. You now need to adjust to each other's wounds from two different perspectives. Notice how each partner can place expectations on how they receive or give validation. While each partner may be looking at this from an opposing side, the result is that early invalidating environments may have used validation as a way to maintain a sense of control or when it suited your caregivers. This made validation something that is now both feared yet needed.

You and your partner offering each other a sense of validation can be done in many ways, including verbally and nonverbally. It's important to understand what type of validation is important to you and your partner, which may tie into each of your specific love languages (Chapman 2010). For example, if you are more anxiously attached, you may find that hearing verbal affirmations of your value and worth are important to you. You may have a need to hear your partner expressing their love for you or complimenting you for putting on their favorite show after a tough day at work.

On the flip side, if you are more avoidantly attached, you may prefer more nonverbal forms of validation, such as spending quality time together. Or you might enjoy acts of service such as having your partner sit next to you while watching your favorite show together.

Notice where you and your partner have similar needs for validation that may manifest differently. For example, an avoidantly attached partner may enjoy spending time sitting on the porch watching the sunset with you but may not be too responsive to a lot of questions on why they seem to be in a bad mood. On the flip side, an anxiously attached partner's first impulse may be to offer their partner attention or encouragement, or to process the day's events—their way of trying to connect and provide validation. Thus, aiming for middle ground and compromising is often necessary.

PRACTICE EXERCISES

The goal of this exercise is to explore different ways you can provide each other validation—either verbally or nonverbally—based on what each of you needs. This can lead to increased empathetic compassion and understanding between you, so you both feel seen, heard, and understood.

1. Grab your journal, or a pen and paper, and if possible, ask your partner to sit down with you.

2. Begin by defining what validation means to each of you.

3. Next, find one situation to explore between you that taps into receiving validation from the other. Do you each have different needs surrounding validation? If so, what are they?

4. How can you both give each other what the other needs in this situation?

5. Explore how you may have received validation in your childhood. Did your parents or caregivers help validate your reality as appreciated and worthy? Did you receive validation from others, such as teachers or friends?

6. Now, write down a few strategies you can use to help each of you feel validated more consistently in your relationship. Use your specific love languages, your unique attachment styles, and whether you each prefer verbal or nonverbal validation, or a combination of them.

If you both choose to complete this on your own, it may be a great opportunity for you to reconnect afterward and exchange each other's answers for deeper insights into what each of you needs.

Now let's turn to respect as another necessary belonging need. As you read, keep in mind how you and your partner show each other love and the ways you both can improve a sense of belongingness between you.

Love

Feeling loved is one of the most basic and fundamental human needs we have. As a child, you likely turned to your primary caregivers to show you that you are valuable and loved. They likely encouraged you to be yourself, embraced your unique quirks, and shared their time and energy with you. Similarly, they may have taught you that you are inherently valuable and worthy, and provided you a foundation that included trust and security. All of these identify love that is necessary for developing a solid sense of self-love and an ability to love those in your life.

Yet, if your earliest experiences did not include these qualities, you may have difficulties with accepting or giving love. If what was modeled for you did not foster a secure attachment toward yourself or the people in your life, then it is only natural to question what love is and whether your partner really loves you. You may have grown up with parents or caregivers who were distant and emotionally disconnected. They may have equated love with things like what career path you chose, what things you own, or what you have accomplished.

You may have become an adult who now pushes others away, even subtly, because you may feel confused or uncertain about how to show vulnerable emotions. You may have an equally hard time accepting emotions from others. Or, you may resonate more with identifying love in all-consuming terms. For instance, love may have been learned as codependency, and any time spent apart from those in your life has become internalized as them not loving you.

Growing up feeling unwanted or unloved can be some of the deepest wounds to overcome, leaving you vulnerable to not knowing what love is or not wanting to experience it. In essence, anyone who experienced an invalidating environment was not being taught love; they were learning what love *isn't.*

A common outcome of growing up feeling unwanted is to attract, and be attracted to, people who are toxic to your sense of self-love and self-respect. In essence, invalidating early environments teach things *backward*—you end up attracting people into your life who do not love you or value you, and who ultimately reinforce your insecurities in feeling unloved and unwanted. These situations are commonly represented in trauma-bonded romantic relationships (briefly discussed in chapter 8). Because this book does not focus on trauma bonds, I want to add another disclaimer here that if you believe you may be experiencing a toxic or abusive relationship, please seek out a professional who can best support your needs.

A feeling of not being loved or wanted is the result of core wounds surrounding early invalidation and disrespect, which you may have carried with you into your romantic relationship. While no caregiver is perfect, and your unique experiences may differ from others, including your partner's experiences, it is important to recognize the impacts of feeling unwanted or unloved. These are perhaps some of the deepest and most profound wounds that a person may carry with them in their life, resulting in many self-defeating behaviors surrounding love and relationships.

Common signs of core wounds surrounding a lack of love:

- High levels of seeking external validation

- Not being told you were wanted, loved, or valued by your family or caregivers

- Inability to express emotions in a healthy and vulnerable way (for example, either shutting down or lashing out)

- Having a shaky sense of self-identity

- Seeing love as something to test or challenge

- Having conflicted feelings about closeness and autonomy

- Failing to meet your own emotional, psychological, or physical self-care needs

- Feeling unseen, unheard, or misunderstood

- Turning to perfectionism or workaholism for validation

- Questioning a person's kindness toward you (for example, looking for agendas)

- A deep sense of feeling useless or worthless

- History of romantic relationships that replay feeling unwanted, unseen, unheard, or unloved

- Feeling as if you do not fit in

- Violating your own needs in order to feel wanted or accepted

- A constant, nagging inner critic

- An inability to relax or feel secure around others in your life

- Patterns associated with creating or seeking chaos within your relationships

- Having learned that love equals pain (and, therefore, turning to self-sabotage)

- Emotional immaturity

Suffice it to say, if you grew up feeling unloved, these wounds can profoundly affect how you see yourself and your ability to love yourself. You may not trust your judgment about meeting a new friend or in choosing an emotionally healthy partner. Or you may wrongly believe that you are not worthy of love or compassion.

On the far end of feeling a lack of self-love, you may have a pattern of subconsciously seeking out romantic relationships that continue triggering your attachment insecurities and unmet needs to feel wanted and loved. However, most common is when a person pushes away or challenges their partner's love because they have not learned how to love themself. A hard truth is that you first have to learn how to appreciate, value, and love yourself before you can accept your partner's love. The flip side is true as well; your partner has to love themself before they can feel secure enough in accepting your love.

Impact on Adult Life

By far, the biggest experiences in feeling a lack of love (both self-love and feeling loved by others) is in your romantic relationship. The reason is simple: your partner should be a safe space for you. They should be someone who provides you a sense of feeling understood, respected, and appreciated. Yet, even if they are providing a consistent

The Anxious-Avoidant Trap

foundation of love and support, it may not be received in a way that resonates for you. Or, if your own core wounds are affecting your sense of self-love, then any love offered cannot be received on a deep and authentic level until you believe you are worthy of receiving it.

A common pattern of not having a solid sense of self-love is in nitpicking how your partner offers you love. In essence, a deep hole that developed from not feeling loved early in your life usually generalizes into a deep hole that affects your ability to recognize and receive love later in your life. For example, instead of appreciating the little things your partner may do for you, such as taking out the trash or holding your hand at the mall, you may focus on things that they need to do to prove their love. This also works in reverse; if your partner does not have a solid sense of self-love, they may find fault in things you do or do not do as reason that you must not love or value them.

Now, let's explore how to deepen your understanding of loving both yourself and your partner.

PRACTICE EXERCISES

Your ability to love yourself may have been negatively impacted from invalidating or abusive environments, or from having experienced rejection or abandonment. An inability to fully love yourself and to authentically believe that you are valued and worthy of receiving love can affect your capacity to trust your partner's love for you. The goal of this exercise is to help you learn to love yourself and notice and trust the ways your partner shows you their love.

Ask your partner to complete this exercise as well. Afterward, exchange responses to help create a deeper understanding of each of your relationship needs surrounding love.

1. Get out your journal, or a sheet of paper, and jot down a definition of what you believe love is, based on your early experiences, as well as with your partner. How did your primary caregivers show you love? In what ways were they lacking in

or incomplete with how they showed love? Did you receive love, validation, and acceptance from another relative or friend?

2. Next, explore what attachment insecurities you may be carrying with you that impact your ability to give or receive love from a place of vulnerability. List each insecurity, and then explore how each of these wounds may be impacting your romantic relationship.

3. Now, write down three patterns you notice within yourself that resonate with each of these insecurities and that result from a lack of feeling good enough for love. What fears do you notice surfacing when you are experiencing feeling unloved? Refer back to chapters 2, 3, 4, and 5 for guidance.

Now, we will turn your attention to learning more about respect as a basic esteem need and how a lack of self-respect or feeling disrespected in your relationships can limit your ability to connect with your partner from a secure base.

Respect

Respect is a necessary esteem need defined as being held in high regard by others, being listened to without interruption or judgment, being shown empathy and compassion, not being gossiped about or triangulated in conversations, and having your personal space and boundaries not violated. When someone respects you, their words and deeds show that they value you as a person. Yet, respect starts with *self*.

If you experienced a harsh upbringing that did not show you that you are worthy of respect, you may have developed a wound that has been carried with you (Maslow 1943, 1962). Narcissistic parenting is a top contributor to the development of many insecurities, including a lack of self-respect, low self-worth, and even experiences of severe chronic depression, anxiety, or trauma-related disorders (Schienle et al. 2015).

For example, if your caregivers were routinely intrusive or invaded your personal space, they were also likely disrespectful of your emotional needs. They may have barged in on you when hanging out with friends or may have taken your door off the hinges to your bedroom when painting the house and "forgot" to put it back on. While these are examples of highly intrusive and narcissistic caregiving, they also include disrespecting your boundaries and personal space as important to your overall well-being.

Disrespectful environments are also invalidating ones. Any rebuttal you may have had about their intrusiveness or failure to give you your personal space may have been met with further dismissals of your feelings or needs. For example, if you complained to your parent for refusing to give you space, they may have responded with "You're too sensitive, get over it" or "If you don't like it, leave."

If you were not shown respect by others, you were also not being taught how to respect *yourself*. As a result, a lack of self-respect may be carried with you, which can be reinforcing to any disrespect received earlier in your life. If you are more prone to an anxious attachment, you may resort to being unduly hard on yourself. Or you may call yourself names for any stress in your life, even if the stress is not your fault and out of your control. These are overt forms of disrespecting yourself. For example, you may blame yourself for your company's failure in providing proper training on a new program being rolled out and internalize the discrepancy as you being incompetent.

On the flip side, if you are more avoidantly attached, a lack of self-respect may be less obvious to others, including to your partner. For example, you may become disgruntled if you have to work in teams during company training on the new program because of a lack of trust that the others will pull their own weight. You may internalize poor training as now having to work harder (to be seen as "perfect") in understanding the new software; this is done in an effort to push away any negative thoughts or insecurities about your work performance or competence on the job. While this may be a more covert form of disrespecting yourself, the outcome is still the same: both anxious and avoidant attachers can feel worthless and resort to being unreasonably disrespectful toward themselves.

Impact on Adult Life

When it comes to your romantic relationship, notice how respect is a two-pronged dynamic. On one end, a lack of respect from your partner can be reinforcing to a lack of self-respect. Yet, a lack of self-respect can make you more hypersensitive to feeling disrespected by your partner. When insecurities are triggered, you not only feel disrespected, you may also begin to invalidate your self-worth. This becomes a circular pattern. Aside from dealing with an attachment insecurity now front and center, you may be misinterpreting your partner's words or actions as being disrespectful toward you or your needs.

Respect is necessary in all relationships. When a relationship lacks respect, it means you are not getting (or giving) the attunement required for meeting each other's needs, feelings, opinions, or beliefs. Sadly, if you or your partner has a history of feeling disrespected, you may not recognize it happening within your romantic relationship. If disrespect was served as "normal" earlier in your life, you may now struggle to recognize where your boundaries start or theirs end, or whether you have been treated poorly.

Common signs of disrespect in a relationship may include putting more time or energy into your career, gym time, or friends—with less emphasis on building and maintaining a healthy bond between you and your partner. Or, you may have become resentful due to feeling disrespected and are now trying to even the score with your partner.

Other signs of disrespect between partners can include:

- Talking for or over the other person

- Pushing your agenda on the other person

- Not being mindful of each person's personal time or space

- Talking about relationship issues to others

- Insulting or lying behind the other person's back

- Ignoring the other person

- Taking things without asking (for example, money, car)

- Violating personal boundaries

- Refusing to discuss a problem or being dismissive about it

- Passive-aggression

- Minimizing or dismissing emotional needs

- Feeling unsafe

- Infidelity or the threat of it

- Breaking a promise

- Imbalance between time alone and time spent together

For example, you may not be mindful of your partner's personal space in allowing them sufficient time to calm down after a disagreement. This is a more common pattern seen in anxious attachment; you may be insistent on wanting an answer or solution to the problem *now* ("pull toward"). This is relatable; it can be difficult sitting in limbo waiting for a resolution if your partner is not wanting to budge.

Yet, it can be equally disrespectful insisting that the problem be resolved immediately or needling your partner for an answer if they are unable or unwilling to give one in the moment ("push away"). As such, a common complaint about anxiously attached partners from more avoidantly attached partners is that they needle them for an answer and are unwilling to give space to cool off or process things, which comes off as disrespectful.

On the flip side, when faced with a disagreement, you may refuse to discuss an issue or may blow it off as unimportant. This is a more common pattern seen in avoidant attachment; you may routinely shut down or walk out ("push away") in the middle of a heated discussion. This is relatable, as it can be very overwhelming having someone expect or demand that you talk if you do not want to.

Yet, this can be incredibly triggering for an anxiously attached partner who may now take chase ("pull toward") by insisting the issue be discussed. This pattern can end up reinforcing the push-pull dynamic between you and your partner instead of a solution that works for both of you. As such, a common complaint about avoidantly attached partners from more anxiously attached partners is that they are unwilling to sit with uncomfortable emotions or communicate effectively during conflict, which comes across as disrespectful.

Next, you'll get a chance to become more aware of patterns of disrespect in your relationship, and how your early experiences may be influencing how you approach feeling respected and respecting your partner.

PRACTICE EXERCISE

Respect is a fundamental need in all relationships. There should be no exception when it comes to your romantic relationship. When you or your partner feels disrespected, it can breed hostility, contempt, or divisiveness between you. It is important to recognize areas in your relationship that may be coming off as disrespectful.

1. To start this exercise, please take out your journal, or a sheet of paper and pen. Begin by defining what self-respect means to you and how you provide yourself a sense of self-respect.

2. Next, explore what respect means to you from those in your life.

3. How was respect taught to you by your caregivers? Friends? Others? If you notice that you were not provided healthy examples of respect earlier in your life, how has this influenced your ability to show yourself respect?

4. Next, label five ways you have felt disrespected by your partner. Explore your reactions toward them. By examining your honest reactions, you can gain insight into whether your behavior is based on self-respect or disrespect. For example, pushing away during an argument may be a go-to pattern that you have turned to since childhood. But, if you still do it in your romantic relationship, is this being respectful to your emotional growth and self-awareness? Is this showing your partner respect?

5. Next, explore how you and your partner can become more mindful of when you each are feeling disrespected. How can you approach it in a healthier way?

6. Last, jot down between five and ten trigger conversations that have led to feeling disrespected in the past with your partner. If these conversations come up, devise an agreed-upon solution that you both can do that is respectful to each of your needs.

Breaking Free from the Anxious-Avoidant Trap

Hopefully, the anxious-avoidant trap is losing its grip on you and you are starting to feel more empowered in your relationships. You now have a better understanding of the origins of unmet belonging and esteem needs, including childhood trauma, prior rejection or abandonment, and narcissistic parenting. These can set the stage for feeling that you do not belong, as well as negatively impact your self-esteem. Ideally, this can now inspire you and your partner to foster the three necessary belonging and esteem needs—validation, love, and respect—within your relationship. In the next chapter, you will integrate everything learned so far by reading a detailed vignette and identifying common attachment insecurities and behavior patterns.

CHAPTER 7

Identifying Common Behavior Patterns

By now, you should have more insight into childhood trauma—both early attachment and environmental. You've learned how traumatic situations can set the stage for developing a more insecure attachment style, specifically one that is more anxious or avoidant. Your attachment style becomes the overarching theme in how you relate to others in your life and in your most intimate relationships. In the previous six chapters, you have been introduced to many concepts, including how perfectionism, parentification, and people-pleasing can start from inconsistent, unpredictable, and unreliable environments. You also learned about the potential negative impacts of experiencing an invalidating environment on your overall sense of self-respect and self-love.

You've explored the necessity of your basic needs being met in your childhood, including the importance of both safety and belonging needs. Hopefully, you've noticed how any perceived gaps in these needs can follow you into your adult life and romantic relationships. Now, you will be given the opportunity to put it all together by applying some of the skills gained and apply them to a fictional couple's relationship problems.

Practicing How to Spot Patterns

A good way to help yourself heal is to practice recognizing and labeling attachment insecurities and common behavior patterns specific to each attachment style. Doing so can serve as a reminder of how to provide each other support that is respectful to each of your unique attachment needs. By sharpening this skill, you can become more astute in determining what you and your partner need within your relationship and what requires your attention and healing.

For example, in a push-pull dynamic, it is necessary to examine what often goes *unspoken* yet may show up in each person's patterns or outward behavior. In other words, it becomes even more important to look at the context of the situation between you and your partner that may be giving clues as to what each of you needs.

This is perhaps most important when considering how a more avoidantly attached partner tends to shut down, or when a more anxiously attached partner becomes more demanding, when either person is feeling overwhelmed or fearful. Thus, by becoming more aware of how to apply what was introduced in earlier chapters into practice, you start learning how to unpack the insecurities and unmet needs that may be influencing your actions toward each other in the moment. You can start by analyzing another couple's relationship, such as the fictional one that follows.

One goal of reading the following vignette is to begin unpacking the patterns you notice in your relationship. As you read the story, keep in mind any similarities or differences you see between the couple's attachment styles, patterned behaviors, and insecurities and those that you and your partner have. It may help to refer to chapters

Identifying Common Behavior Patterns

1 through 6 as you analyze the story, particularly in relation to basic safety, belonging, and esteem needs; early trauma; invalidating environments; and anything else that may have shaped attachment styles.

• *Jeannie and Jonathan*

Jeannie is a forty-year-old academic consultant who makes her own hours and schedule. She is dating Jonathan, a forty-two-year-old pilot. They have been together for two and half years and have a comfortable relationship. Jeannie likes that Jonathan is gone a couple weeks out of the month because it allows her to focus on her work. She admits she is perfectionistic in her job and that it takes precedence in her life. Jonathan likes that he travels often for work because he gets to see new places. He wishes that Jeannie would be open to working remotely and traveling with him, as he often feels worried about their relationship when they're not together. While he understands that she has a lot of responsibilities in keeping on top of her career obligations, he does miss her when he is gone for work and routinely calls her when he settles into his hotel.

Jeannie, on the other hand, actually feels closer to Jonathan when he is not at home. She admits that when he is more accessible to her it tends to irritate her. Jeannie says that their relationship is "good" but knows she has difficulty in expressing her needs and feelings to Jonathan. Jonathan says he loves Jeannie and asked her to marry him a few months ago. He was disappointed to learn that she is not ready for that kind of commitment, which has made him feel more anxious in the relationship.

Jeannie grew up in a narcissistic home where both parents were highly successful and demanded nothing less than that from her. Her childhood was lonely; her brother was shipped off to boarding school to "behave," and her parents did not offer any emotional support for her. The only sense of attention or validation she received was when she was excelling in her schoolwork, as it made her parents look good to their colleagues.

Jeannie says that she had a great home growing up but never felt safe or wanted. Her father was prone to rages when dealing with work-related stress, and her mother would get drunk from too many cocktails every night. She admits she has struggled with depression since she was a teenager but that academics have been an outlet for her. When she was accepted into a prestigious college to study business, her parents cut her off financially because her choice of study was not their choice for her. Jeannie resorted to working two jobs to make ends meet while in college. Now, as a successful self-employed consultant, she has not spoken to her parents in more than a decade.

Jonathan grew up in a middle-class home. His parents met in college and married shortly after graduating. His mother is a teacher for a local community college, and his father owns his own small accounting firm. Jonathan has two siblings who work at their dand's office. He says some of his favorite childhood memories were when his parents would pile everyone into the car and go camping. Jonathan states that his parents are wonderful, that they provided a safe homelife for him and his siblings, and that he loves them deeply.

He says that his mother was diagnosed with an anxiety disorder after his youngest sibling was born but that she manages it through a healthy lifestyle. Jonathan claims that there is nothing that stands out as traumatic in his childhood but that he did have a couple "bad relationships" before Jeannie. One ex-girlfriend cut off their relationship after she took a new job, and that experience left him feeling "like nothing I did was ever good enough" for her. Another ex-girlfriend abruptly dumped Jonathan without explanation. He admits that he has had a difficult time moving past both experiences due to the betrayal and lack of closure.

Unpacking the Dynamics

Based on this story, there is a lot you can unpack about each partner individually, as well as how their early experiences may be overshadowing their relationship. Let's explore the dynamics within the vignette.

Jeannie's presumed attachment style: Based on the above information, Jeannie displays signs of a more avoidant attachment style, which include a high tendency for self-reliance, feelings of emotional disconnection, need for personal space, preferring when Jonathan is gone for work, tendency to avoid emotional intimacy, propensity for workaholism and perfectionism, and indifference about marriage. All patterns tilt toward being more avoidantly attached.

Jonathan's presumed attachment style: Jonathan appears to be a little more anxiously attached. He is able to express that he loves his parents deeply and that they talk weekly. He states that his parents are very proud and supportive of his career choice, even if they may have wanted him to work at the family business. Jonathan's childhood memories are met with fondness and make him happy, and his parents and siblings seem to have a relatively stable family relationship. His early homelife appears to be safe and secure; his basic needs for safety and emotional security were met. However, he has a history of toxic romantic relationships prior to Jeannie that may be influencing his ability to remain present with her. Jonathan openly expresses loving her and wanting to marry her, but he also confesses that her refusal to marry him has triggered painful memories from past relationships. He understands and respects that Jeannie requires more time to herself than he does, but admits he becomes more anxious when not together.

Attachment insecurities for Jeannie: Jeannie states that she is a perfectionist within her career, which may have resulted from her invalidating early environment that was riddled with unrealistic expectations. Her parents demanded that she perform and achieve as they did, and ultimately cut her out of their lives when she chose a different career path. In her romantic relationship with Jonathan, Jeannie struggles with a need to be perfect, which may lead her to feel a compulsion in wanting to control every detail in the relationship (for example, whether she chooses to travel with him; whether she accepts his marriage proposal). Her difficulty with emotions may prompt her to continue choosing her career over her romantic relationship as safer than getting married and risking feeling controlled or stifled in her autonomy.

Attachment insecurities for Jonathan: Jonathan seems more securely attached around his family but appears to be more anxiously attached in romantic relationships. Because he is dating someone who seems more avoidantly attached, he may be feeling emotionally needy in the relationship. This, over time, may trigger insecurities in his self-esteem or self-worth. Similarly, Jonathan admits to a history of toxic relationships which makes him feel more anxious around Jeannie, especially when she seems fine not spending time together.

Fear of intimacy for Jeannie: Fears of being engulfed in a relationship can cause a person to shut down or push away. In Jeannie's case, she feels closer to Jonathan when he is gone for work, meaning that it is safe for her to miss him when he is not in close proximity to her. Instead of giving Jonathan her emotional energy, she turns to workaholism as a safe way of avoiding intimacy with him; she focuses on things that are less threatening to her independence or vulnerability.

Fear of intimacy for Jonathan: Jonathan displays some fears of abandonment because of his romantic relationship history. While he tries to respect Jeannie's space, it triggers more anxiety in him due to exes who abruptly left the relationship for a job or for someone else without warning. He may feel that Jeannie is reevaluating the relationship or spending time with someone else when they are not together.

Communication issues for Jeannie: As more avoidantly attached, Jeannie is prone to ignoring or minimizing her feelings. She gives a rather generic response in saying she is not ready for the commitment of marriage but does not provide Jonathan much else to go on. If she does have a more avoidant attachment style, she also likely has difficulty with taking the initiative in conversations, including more emotionally vulnerable ones, such as talking about marriage.

Communication issues for Jonathan: Because Jonathan appears to be anxiously attached, he may benefit from becoming a little more assertive in expressing his emotional needs for connection with Jeannie. He may also benefit from learning how to feel more confident and comfortable with himself when they are not together.

Feeling misunderstood for Jeannie: Jeannie appears to have deep wounds that surround feeling misunderstood that date back to her narcissistic upbringing. Jeannie's childhood did not seem happy or safe, and misunderstandings may have been a common theme, especially with regard to her career choice and subsequently being disowned by her parents. In her relationship with Jonathan, she may feel misunderstood in pushing away or in choosing to remain autonomous as rejecting Jonathan's love. Or he may assume her inability to express her emotions in a healthy way as her being narcissistic, especially given her childhood.

Feeling misunderstood for Jonathan: Because Jonathan appears more anxiously attached, he may feel misunderstood when turning toward Jeannie for love and connection, and having her push away while turning to her work. This pattern can be reinforcing to his fears of being replaced or abandoned, thus re-triggering his anxiousness within the relationship. This is something that should be addressed and for which a solution is found (see "Recommended Support," below).

Safety seeds for Jeannie: Jeannie admitted that she did not always feel safe in her home because her father was prone to rage when having a bad day at work and her mother was an alcoholic. If her mother was not supportive or protective of her need for safety, this can exacerbate feeling unsafe in her own home, as well as feeling a sense of betrayal by her mother. Similarly, her brother was sent to boarding school to "behave," which can trigger a fear that if she does something wrong, she too will be shipped away. While it sounds as if she grew up privileged, within her home there was chaos with two narcissistic caregivers who were demanding and invalidating of her needs.

Safety needs for Jonathan: Jonathan appears to have parents who met his safety needs, including the need for consistency, predictability, and reliability. However, either Jonathan did not tell his parents about his prior romantic relationship history, or they may have chosen to stay out of it, leaving him feeling unsure of how to handle this situation with Jeannie. There appears to be no evidence of abuse, narcissistic parenting, or an invalidating early environment that could have compromised his sense of feeling secure within his home and family. His overall sense of feeling safe appears to have spread into his adult life, as he still receives weekly calls from his parents who check in on him. However, his past romantic relationships seem to have left him feeling a lack of trust and emotionally unsafe. While he displays predictability, consistency, and reliability in how he approaches Jeannie, her indifference toward him may trigger his insecurities surrounding feeling emotionally unsafe or questioning if he can trust her in the relationship.

Core attachment insecurities for Jeannie: Suffice it to say, it appears that Jeannie has experienced a high level of narcissistic abuse, attachment insecurities, abandonment, and rejection. While Jeannie did not mention any physical abuse in her childhood, her parents appear to be very invalidating, emotionally negligent, and demanding of her. For example, Jeannie's parents are both high-powered doctors. They only offered her validation when she was performing or achieving in school, and impulsively cut her out of their lives for choosing a career they did not approve of. Similarly, her brother was shipped off to boarding school, so she likely experienced a sense of physical abandonment with him gone. Jeannie likely carries deep wounds in feeling unworthy. These wounds, as well as her unmet needs for belonging (see "Belonging and Esteem Needs for Jeannie," below), identify core deficits in her ability to love and appreciate herself, as well as in her ability to feel emotionally safe and vulnerable with Jonathan.

Core attachment insecurities for Jonathan: While he did not seem to experience any core traumatic insecurities growing up, he has a history of rejection, betrayal, and abandonment in his romantic relationships with partners who were likely narcissistic. Feeling rejected, used, or immediately replaced with someone else likely has affected his overall sense of safety and belongingness (see "Safety Needs" and "Belonging and Esteem Needs").

Belonging and esteem needs for Jeannie: Jeannie appears to have very deep wounds relating to a lack of feeling that she belonged within her family of origin. Her parents did not seem to offer her any validation, outside of her school performance. Similarly, their idea of love appears to be self-centered, egotistical, and conditional on her and her brother's behavior, rather than on who they are as unique people and as members of the family. Additionally, she did not seem to have respect from her parents, as they easily shunned her when she chose a different path for herself.

Belonging and esteem needs for Jonathan: Jonathan likely has very real unmet needs to feel validated, loved, and respected within his relationship with Jeannie. He appears to have a lot of love to give her; he

The Anxious-Avoidant Trap

seems validating toward her needs and respectful of her needing personal space. However, she is less receptive to his needs because of insecurities and early traumatic experiences impacting her ability to give and receive validation, respect, and love within their relationship.

Their story is a perfect example of how unhealed insecurities can—and usually do—negatively impact a person's ability to remain present, grounded, and emotionally available for themself and their partner until they start the healing process.

Recommended Support

Given that Jeannie and Jonathan have been dating for two and a half years, it may be a good idea for them to seek guidance with a relationship counselor who can provide them support. Because Jonathan appears more anxiously attached in romantic relationships, it is necessary that any relationship counseling help provide actionable tools and skills to help promote his autonomy and self-worth. Jeannie needs to be more receptive in helping him feel wanted and loved, as it can be challenging for a more anxiously attached person to be in a relationship with a more avoidantly attached one.

Finding ways to balance her need for personal space with his desire for validation and closeness is critical in helping make their relationship work. It is also important that each of them address feeling misunderstood. For example, it may help Jonathan to speak up more and ask for clarification regarding Jeannie's refusal to get married, along with validation that she still loves him. It may help Jeannie to begin practicing putting herself in his (emotional) shoes, in order to boost empathy and compassion. It is also important that Jeannie be willing to seek support and be on board with learning skills for a healthier work-life balance with Jonathan. Individual therapy may also be a good choice for her, so she can unpack her painful childhood and find support in healing.

Now, grab a pen and paper, and see how you and your partner can unpack your relationship using the same prompts as in Jonathan and Jeannie's vignette.

PRACTICE EXERCISE

The vignette was designed to help you notice common patterns within an anxious-avoidant relationship and how they can play out. Let's start by exploring these questions in writing:

1. If Jonathan were more *securely* attached, how may his communication toward Jeannie change when it comes to expressing his emotional needs for connection without fearing she will leave him as his past partners did? How could Jonathan gain more self-confidence while not being reliant on Jeannie's approval? How may his newfound self-confidence help him concerning his relationship with Jeannie?

2. If Jeannie were more *securely* attached, how could she approach Jonathan regarding her needs to feel safe, validated, and understood? Given that she grew up privileged but from a highly narcissistic family with alcoholism, rage, and betrayal as the norm, where may be a good place for her to start talking with a professional? How may she approach Jonathan about her needs and fears?

3. Now, write down your life story, including your caregiver relationships and your early environment. Include your childhood experiences and any emotional wounds that may have shaped your attachment style and your romantic relationship.

4. Then, ask your partner to do the same. The goal is to integrate a cohesive account of your and your partner's stories by identifying overall themes in your romantic relationship and in each of your unique upbringings.

5. Last, use the eight prompts above—attachment style, insecurities, fear of intimacy, communication, feeling misunderstood, safety needs, and belonging and esteem needs—to begin creating a richer picture of each other's relationship needs.

Breaking Free from the Anxious-Avoidant Trap

You have now gotten some practice in exploring and unpacking certain patterns that may be replaying in your relationship based on the sample vignette. Hopefully, you are now starting to feel much more confident in learning how to break free from an anxious-avoidant trap with your partner by continuing to use the skills provided. You will now turn to building intimacy with your partner in chapter 8.

CHAPTER 8

Establishing and Maintaining Intimacy

Most things in life can be placed along a continuum, and there is no exception when it comes to romantic relationships. It is important to recognize where your relationship may be falling along this continuum with regard to building and maintaining intimacy, and in practicing healthy conflict resolution. We all want healthy and connected relationships. We all want to feel seen, heard, understood, and respected by our partner. We also want to minimize disagreements in our relationship that can lead to tension and anger.

However, there is a common misconception that relationships with a high level of intimacy are also void of disagreement or conflict. This is untrue. All relationships have conflict and will experience an inevitable rupture at one time or another. *How* we choose to approach these issues and resolve them is what identifies healthy and satisfying relationships.

Common Relationship Types

There are four common types of romantic relationships: *healthy relationships, anxious-avoidant relationships, toxic relationships,* and *trauma-bonded relationships,* as can be seen on this continuum:

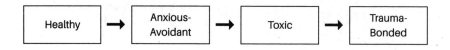

Each of these four types will inevitably experience conflict, yet the intensity and frequency of conflict is key in recognizing the differences between them, as you will learn about next.

Healthy Relationships

The following list touches on the most important traits for a healthy and sustainable relationship with your partner. While it is not exhaustive, it includes some of the most critical traits for cultivating healthy connection:

- Trust
- Self-awareness
- Safety
- Authenticity
- Interdependence
- Responsibility/accountability
- Honesty
- Transparency

- Friendship
- Commitment
- Self-respect
- Respect for partner
- Intimacy
- Passion
- Collaboration
- Consistency
- Predictability
- Reliability
- Healthy communication
- Individual space
- Solution-focused conflict
- Balance of power
- Self-acceptance
- Solid sense of self-identity

When a relationship is deemed healthy, it means that both partners have a high level of self-awareness and are cognizant of any insecurities they may have carried into the relationship. Healthy relationships also include each partner addressing any dysfunctional patterns that may be replaying in their life or relationship as a result of these wounds. Healthy relationships are respectful of each partner's individuality and needs. They allow for space without someone feeling threatened or jealous, and they allow each partner to show up as their authentic self.

When a relationship is considered healthy, disagreements are kept to the issue at hand, without old arguments being dredged up. There is a deep appreciation for each other and a high level of respect. Trust and honesty are foundational in a healthy relationship, as well as upholding relationship norms and boundaries, as identified by each partner.

Anxious-Avoidant Relationships

One word I often hear that defines an anxious-avoidant trap is "unsatisfying." The relationship is not trauma bonded. However, without both partners making an emotional investment into cultivating healthier ways of building and maintaining intimacy, the relationship can devolve into a toxic one, or a trauma bond.

Signs of Distress

Push-pull dynamics within an anxious-avoidant relationship include these obvious signs of relational distress:

- Opposing attachment styles

- Opposing needs regarding intimacy

- Constant reassurance-seeking

- Emotional dependence

- Fear of abandonment

- Fear of engulfment

Establishing and Maintaining Intimacy

- Difficulties with remaining present or expressing vulnerability

- Nitpicking

- Bringing up the past during arguments

- Manipulative behavior to feel seen or heard

- Pacifying a partner to avoid arguments (which typically ends up making arguments worse)

- Jealousy or possessiveness

- Emotional distance

- Comparing self to others

- Anxiety that is often intensified by the relationship

- Trust issues, especially when not together (for example, at work, with friends, and so forth)

- Poor conflict resolution

- Miscommunication, either in excesses or with deficits

- Passive aggression or sarcasm

- Overstepping of personal space

- Moderate number of disagreements without a solution

- Low to moderately intense arguments

- One or both partners have history of childhood traumatic events

If your relationship is deemed an anxious-avoidant one, you likely notice difficulties with trust that originated in childhood and that

135

affect your ability to feel fully vulnerable and intimate with your partner. Many equate a push-pull dynamic within their relationship as feeling defensive or constantly looking for the first slight in their partner's behavior as validation they are not loved.

When a push-pull dynamic is in effect, intimacy and healthy communication between you and your partner suffer. Poor communication often surrounds each other's needs, and poor conflict resolution can leave issues either up in the air or repeatedly brought up. Many who find themselves in a push-pull dynamic did not receive much emotional support growing up, which may have created a desperation to feel seen and heard, or a compulsion to remain independent and shut down. While both anxious and avoidant attachers want intimacy and love, each has different ways of approaching it based on attachment style patterns. These patterns can be reinforcing to your unmet needs and fears.

As you move along the relationship continuum, one thing you may notice is that there is a negative correlation between intimacy and toxicity: the higher the level of toxicity, the lower the level of intimacy.

Toxic Relationships

When a relationship becomes toxic, it cannot be salvaged. Toxic relationships are aligned with many of the same patterns seen in trauma-bonded relationships and carry the following common signs:

- Control, either coercively or overtly

- High levels of manipulation (for example, trying to one-up the other person for their own gains)

- Blatant disrespect

- Denial and deflection

- Blaming or projection

- Fast-tracking the relationship with physical intimacy

- Gaslighting

- Infidelity

- Stonewalling

- High levels of criticism during arguments

- Repetition compulsion, or seeking out relationships that replay early traumatic events

- Lack of security

- Inconsistency

- Unreliability or not being able to count on your partner

- Secrecy between partners

- High number of disagreements without a solution

- High-intensity arguments

- Triangulating family or friends in arguments or trying to divide

Trauma-Bonded Relationships

The type of relationship that falls along the farthest end of the continuum is a *trauma bond*. If you believe you and your partner are in a trauma-bonded relationship (often called "addictive" because of the intense highs and lows that involve a chemical hook), it is important to recognize that these relationships cannot be sustained; they need to end for you to heal. Trauma-bonded relationships confuse intensity and passion with love and intimacy. It is this intensity, or all-encompassing physical chemistry—along with the passionate, dramatic, or exciting highs and lows—that hook a person into believing it is love.

These relationships are defined by most (or all) signs of a toxic relationship, plus patterns of abuse, betrayal, isolation, control, unpredictability, a very high number of disagreements within a specific time frame without a solution, extremely intense arguments, and repeated violations to personal safety.

If this describes your relationship, you should seek out a professional who can support your needs and help you heal (Dutton and Painter 1993).

Threats to Developing Intimacy

Now that you have learned about four types of romantic relationships and their common behaviors, you should have a clearer picture of how to recognize key patterns within your relationship. You should also be able to identify the push-pull dynamics seen in an anxious-avoidant trap that may be negatively affecting intimacy. There are three defining factors that distinguish unavoidable conflict seen in healthy relationships from conflict seen in a push-pull dynamic, toxic relationship, or trauma bond. All three can erode intimacy. They are: the *frequency* of the conflict, the *intensity* of the conflict, and whether each partner is *solution-focused*.

Frequency of Conflict

Frequency is the amount, or number of times, something occurs within a given time period, such as per twenty-four hours or per week. Within healthy relationships, there is a low number of arguments within a specified amount of time. This should not suggest that people in healthy relationships never argue; they do. However, arguments do not define the context of communication in a healthy relationship.

When there is a high frequency of conflict, disagreements are happening often within a specified amount of time. For example, arguments may include the *same* argument being brought up every day or every week, or several *different* topics within the same time frame. With a high frequency of arguing, the emotional or physical distance between you and your partner grows or becomes more obvious, from one argument to the next.

When exploring how often you and your partner disagree about something that may be causing a roadblock with intimacy, it is important to include the following:

- **A weekly log of arguments.** If, on average, you and your partner argue a couple times a month, start a weekly log to track when arguments occur (for example, on weekends, at night before bed, and so forth). If you notice that you are arguing frequently, it may be a good idea to break down each day into *hourly* segments; doing so will give you a richer understanding of the frequency of your disagreements.

- **What the argument was about.** This can provide you both insight into patterns that may be occurring, such as having disagreements about the same issue.

Intensity of Conflict

Intensity refers to the impact of the conflict, or how all-encompassing your thoughts, feelings, or beliefs are surrounding the topic being argued. Hair-trigger reactions likely indicate an intense argument. With high-intensity arguing, you may notice it takes you or your partner longer to calm down afterward. Or, you may notice that you

The Anxious-Avoidant Trap

or they are avoiding intimacy at all costs, including possibly sleeping on the sofa or leaving the house. Low-intensity arguments may include bickering or nitpicking, whereas highly intense arguments often include criticisms, deflections or denials, projection or blaming, stonewalling, and defensiveness. You may also feel increased tension or the "walking on eggshells" feeling, whereby you may be afraid to say anything out of fear that it may jump-start another argument.

When examining the intensity of your and your partner's disagreements, it is recommended to use a rating scale.

1	2	3	4	5	6	7	8	9	10
Healthy		Anxious- Avoidant				Toxic		Trauma- Bonded	

Out of a maximum intensity rating of 10, healthy relationships often toggle around 1 or 2. An anxious-avoidant trap will typically hover around 3 to 5, with an average of 4. A moderate intensity of 5 may include constant nitpicking, bickering, eye rolls, passive-aggression, and so forth. Toxic relationships usually hover around 6 to 8, and trauma-bonded relationships typically range from 8 to 10. An intensity of 10 can include constant stonewalling, yelling or screaming, physical abuse, blaming or projection, triangulating, testing each other, denial or deflection, power imbalance, isolation, intense criticism, and so forth. Because you and your partner are the best judges of how your disagreements typically play out, it is important to be honest in your overall scale.

Whether Conflict Is Solution-Focused

The final threat to intimacy is when arguments are not *solution-focused*. In healthy relationships where intimacy is built and sustained, there is respectful communication, compromise between

Establishing and Maintaining Intimacy

both partners, and consistency in how each of you responds. Solutions regarding a disagreement are achievable, and both partners end up being satisfied with the solution reached. On the flip side, in anxious-avoidant relationships, toxic relationships, and trauma-bonded relationships, you will notice varying degrees of arguing, without resolution.

Thus, one of the most important skills to learn is how to recognize the patterns that may be negatively affecting intimacy and maintaining a stalemate in your relationship. Solutions explored should include those that are:

- **Functional**, meaning the solution is doable and easily implemented; and

- **Fair**, meaning there is no power imbalance and one partner does not have to give up their needs.

Now that you've learned about threats to intimacy—including the frequency of the conflict, the intensity of the conflict, and whether each partner is solution-focused—you're invited to do the next exercise.

PRACTICE EXERCISE

This exercise is designed to help you recognize how common signs of an anxious-avoidant trap have been influencing your relationship and limiting intimacy. Recall that people stuck in an anxious-avoidant trap often report feeling *unsatisfied* or that their relationship is somehow missing something. This happens because there are opposing viewpoints on intimacy and autonomy. Now let's explore the unique push-pull dynamics within your relationship.

1. Please grab your journal or a sheet of paper and a pen.

2. Next, choose two or three traits from the list of "Signs of Distress" earlier in this chapter that you feel are impacting

The Anxious-Avoidant Trap

intimacy between you and your partner. Ask your partner to do the same.

3. For each trait you list, give an example. For instance, if you chose "jealousy or possessiveness," first define what it looks like in action, such as, "I tend to feel very insecure when my partner is on their phone, and so I want to see what they are doing or whom they are talking to."

4. Next, explore how each of the traits you listed are impacted by the three factors that affect intimacy: frequency of arguments, intensity of arguments, and lack of solution. For example, for *frequency* you might write: "About twice a week, I find myself getting jealous or possessive of my partner being on their phone. I notice the pattern happens mostly on weekends when they have more free time. The argument usually starts when I notice they have been on their phone for at least half an hour, and I start questioning what they are doing."

5. For *intensity*, you might write: "I would say these arguments are about a 4 in intensity. I know I get angry and sometimes yell at them to get off their phone or roll my eyes when I see them on their phone. I am now starting to recognize that I feel left out and jealous that they are giving more attention to their phone than me."

6. Ask your partner to do the same.

7. Then, exchange lists. As you read what your partner wrote, remain as objective as possible; don't allow any insecurities to affect this exercise. Remember, you both are on the same team and can find a workable solution together.

8. With your partner, discuss *solutions*. Start by discussing your feelings using "I" statements; avoid accusations and insults. You may choose to write down ahead of time what you want to say and stick to that script.

Establishing and Maintaining Intimacy

Using the same example, some functional and fair solutions can include:

- Having designated cell phone time during the day when phone use is allowed without judgment, questions, or interference. This allows for you to sit with your own insecurities and challenge them while supporting trust and personal space in your relationship.

- Balancing cell phone use with time spent together without cell phone use.

- Recognizing where your personal insecurities are and challenging any limiting self-beliefs or fears that may be maintaining this argument. For example, have you been cheated on in a past relationship? That old betrayal and your pain surrounding it may be spilling into your current relationship. It may not be your current partner as much as it is your past experiences in having been hurt.

- Putting away cell phones and not using them in the bedroom or during dinner. These can be designated times to build intimacy, without the distraction of technology.

- Being patient with implementing these new boundaries, as any change will take time and effort on both your parts.

Now, we are going to explore three common types of intimacy in romantic relationships and how to begin increasing intimacy with your partner.

Common Types of Intimacy

What do you feel is the quality of intimacy between you and your partner? Do you feel that you both have a high level of intimacy in your relationship? What types of intimacy are there? Are you aware of any fears surrounding exploring intimacy with your partner? These are common questions many professionals may ask their clients when it comes to intimacy with a partner.

One of the biggest impacts on intimacy is *fear*. Fears surrounding intimacy can result in a push-pull dynamic because of differing attachment needs between anxious and avoidant partners. If your fears surround being left behind or rejected by your partner, you may be living with a more anxious attachment style.

For example, if growing up you experienced your parents divorcing, and after their divorce you no longer heard from the parent who moved out, this may have left you feeling unworthy of protection or love, or that all people in your life will eventually leave you. In time, these feelings and misbeliefs could solidify into a fear of abandonment or rejection.

On the flip side, if you feel trapped when your partner or others try to be emotionally or physically close to you, or you feel an all-consuming impulse to run, you may be more avoidantly attached and living with a longstanding fear of engulfment.

For example, if growing up your caregivers were invalidating to you, downplayed a problem you had, or showed anger toward you when you were seeking their help, these experiences may have left you feeling as if you could not reliably count on others for support. In time, these feelings and misbeliefs could solidify into feeling tense, uncertain, or even disgusted by someone in your life who is turning to you for intimacy.

There are several common types of intimacy seen within romantic relationships that can be negatively impacted by a fear of abandonment or engulfment surfacing, including *emotional, physical,* and *intellectual*. Because intimacy is foundational for a relationship, when a fear of intimacy arises, it can destabilize the relationship and impact its quality. Suffice it to say, an inability to be vulnerable around those closest to you in your life can create friction between anyone involved.

When it comes to intimacy issues surfacing within an anxious-avoidant relationship, they likely take center stage. The quality of your relationship hinges on how satisfying the intimacy is. Higher levels of satisfaction with intimacy typically indicate a more committed and emotionally healthy partnership.

Let's look at three common types of intimacy and what may happen if intimacy needs go unmet within your romantic relationship. While these forms of intimacy do not compose an exhaustive list, they are the most commonly sought within romantic relationships.

Emotional Intimacy

Emotional intimacy includes the degree to which both you and your partner are able to self-disclose, allow for vulnerability, and feel emotionally safe in each other's company. When you feel safe (see chapter 5) to be emotionally intimate with your partner, you're able to discuss hot-topic issues such as fears, childhood trauma, finances, and plans for your future together. Emotional intimacy also includes being mindful of each other's love languages and how you each respond to experiencing love, as well as your thoughts and feelings regarding any self-awareness moments.

Emotional intimacy is the bedrock for a connected and authentic relationship, irrespective of whether the person is your family member, friend, or your partner. When there is a breakdown in emotional intimacy, it can create issues in communication between those involved. For example, you or your partner may resort to name calling, stonewalling, or defensiveness when feeling unseen, unheard, or misunderstood (Gottman 1995). Less obvious signs of a breakdown in emotional intimacy may include resorting to surface-level and superficial conversations (for example, keeping it to chores or work-related questions), or superficial experiences such as weekends out with friends. Shallow conversations and experiences limit the opportunity for increasing emotional intimacy and maintain what feels like an invisible wall between you and your partner.

The Anxious-Avoidant Trap

If you are more anxiously attached, you may see emotional intimacy as the gold standard when it comes to bonding with your partner. Many who are anxiously attached are desperate for a deep and fulfilling connection with their avoidant partner. It is perfectly natural to want to bond with your partner and experience meaningful connection with them. Yet, it can feel all-consuming for a more avoidantly attached partner who likely does not know how to provide you the level of emotional intimacy you want.

Ironically, this intense desire for emotional intimacy can trigger becoming hypersensitive to your partner's responses and to reading into the situation. Now, instead of your partner providing you the reassurance you are seeking in knowing you are loved and valued, they may shut down. Shutting down can be triggering to your fears of abandonment. You may become suspicious or accusatory if they pull away, or you may be hyperfocused on their behavior as validation that they do not love you. Or, you may become demanding in knowing what they are thinking or feeling.

If you are more avoidantly attached, emotional intimacy is often seen as something you simultaneously want but fear. Many who are more avoidantly attached are drawn to the intensity and newness of the early stages of a relationship. Yet, they often start pumping the brakes when the relationship becomes more emotionally intimate.

It is natural to want time to yourself and to prioritize your autonomy. Everyone needs space and time to themselves, and needing extra time may be something that is necessary for your growth and healing. If more avoidantly attached, you may feel your wall goes up when your partner tries to become more emotionally close to you or asks you loaded questions surrounding your investment to them and the relationship. You may feel that you are being nagged or that your partner is putting too many expectations on you, such that the relationship feels staged and no longer organic.

Or, you may become visibly irritated or short tempered when your efforts at feeling closer to your partner are questioned. This dynamic can be especially common if your partner is more anxiously attached, as their attachment dynamic becomes hyperactivated to any changes in your behavior. Ironically, it is this discomfort toward emotional intimacy that can be reinforcing to deactivating strategies around your partner. Now, instead of your partner offering you a safe space for allowing you to gradually become closer and more vulnerable with them, they may become angry, demanding, or clingy. This can create further distance between you both—and retrigger feelings of engulfment.

Physical Intimacy

When you hear the words "physical intimacy," if you are like many, your thoughts may go right to sexual intimacy. However, while sexual intimacy is a form of physical intimacy, it is much more nuanced than just sex. Physical intimacy also involves proximity, such as how close you and your partner are to each other when walking together in public or when sitting on the couch at home. Physical intimacy also includes affectionate touch such as a gentle pat on the back, a hug, a kiss, a playful ruffling of their hair, holding hands, a massage, or snuggling up to each other.

As with all intimacy needs, there has to be a solid foundation of security in knowing that your partner's touch is consistent. It must also be in tune with each other's comfort levels. For example, if you are more avoidantly attached, you may not like to cuddle in bed at night with your partner. Cuddling may make you feel physically trapped and so you push away to reestablish your autonomy. On the flip side, if you are more anxiously attached, you may have a very real need to feel your partner close to you in bed to provide a sense of security and safety.

These opposing physical intimacy needs can create a rift in the relationship, whereby each partner feels they are not getting their needs met. This can create anger, frustration, or even contempt. Physical intimacy is necessary for a healthy and fulfilling romantic relationship. Yet, when a breakdown occurs surrounding each partner's physical intimacy needs, it can leave both partners feeling misunderstood and at a stalemate.

If you are more anxiously attached, you may be at a higher risk of settling on physical intimacy in your relationship. If this is the case, physical intimacy may ultimately replace any emotional intimacy you want with your partner. You may believe that if you are not getting the validation and emotional connection you seek with them outside of the bedroom, you may as well receive it through physical intimacy in the bedroom. Yet, this can leave you feeling ashamed for having needs or in developing misbeliefs about yourself that your needs are somehow unrealistic.

This may cause you to push your needs aside for the sake of the relationship (for example, taking on a people-pleasing role) while increasing feelings of resentment toward your partner. This, in turn, may lead to a pattern of using physical intimacy as a way of seducing your partner so you can feel closer to them while helping bridge any missing emotional needs. Or, you may use it manipulatively to gain momentary control over your partner's attention, such as diverting their attention away from their cell phone in order to feel wanted. When intimacy becomes staged, these patterns can ultimately place you and your partner at an increased risk of feeling *less* emotionally and physically connected—and more dissatisfied within your relationship.

If you are more avoidantly attached, you may feel one of two common ways about physical intimacy: more comfortable with casual "situationships," or not comfortable with physical intimacy in general. Casual encounters can be seen as less threatening to your sense of autonomy and independence because there are no emotional expectations on the relationship, and physical intimacy typically remains the only form of intimacy experienced.

Some with a more avoidant attachment style may not feel comfortable expressing closeness or vulnerability, which can include any form of physical intimacy. For example, you may be fine walking a couple feet ahead of your partner when out in public and may not hold their hand. However, if your partner is more anxiously attached, walking independently of them without holding their hand will likely be experienced as dismissive of the relationship. They may become demanding or may try taking your hand in an attempt to have their needs met. However, their efforts may backfire by coming across as pushy or overbearing, causing you to recoil further away from them.

Intellectual Intimacy

Intellectual intimacy may not be as well-known as other forms of intimacy, but it is just as necessary for a healthy and successful partnership. When you have intellectual intimacy with your partner, it is based on being in sync with each other enough to discuss any topics that spark a healthy debate or deep conversation. With intellectual intimacy, both partners are free to feel safe enough discussing academics, politics, value systems, or polarizing issues without feeling shamed or lost in the conversation. Hence, intellectual intimacy also includes healthy banter between partners who feel they are with their intellectual equal.

When there is a mismatch in intellectual equality, it can leave one or both partners feeling unfilled in the relationship. Conversations may be reduced to superficial chitchat, or they may hover around less stimulating or engaging topics where boredom is common. However, when there is a rich level of intellectual intimacy between you and your partner, you are excited to learn from each other and are open to exchanging knowledge that sparks the other person's interest.

If you live with a more avoidant attachment style, you may be at a greater risk of intellectualizing your emotions by focusing on logic and facts to avoid emotional intimacy. Because those who are more avoidantly attached tend to feel easily overwhelmed surrounding emotions and emotional sensitivity, using the defense mechanism of intellectualization may help them feel less emotionally vulnerable in the moment.

For example, you and your partner may be chatting about a topic that taps into an opportunity to emotionally bond, such as your partner wanting your feedback on how you healed from a painful breakup or what you would do if feeling emotionally unfulfilled at work. However, if you are more avoidantly attached, you may instead focus on how to fix the situation instead of tapping into your emotional experiences surrounding it. You may offer up unsolicited advice on how to look for signs to avoid a potential toxic relationship or give tips on how they can polish up their résumé for a new job. While these may offer up strategies on how to proceed with something, they can leave your partner feeling intellectually or emotionally unfulfilled.

When Intimacy Needs Collide

It is a common misbelief that if you are anxiously attached, you are fine with intimacy. Actually, anyone who is anxiously attached may put their efforts into trying to push aside their fears of rejection or abandonment by hyperfocusing on *togetherness* with their partner and confusing it as intimacy. This togetherness may be hiding a deeper need for control by insisting on spending more time with your partner or knowing where they are at all times.

While a sense of control can make you feel momentarily empowered in the relationship, it does not allow you to be fully present or vulnerable regarding true intimacy. The reality is that if your energy is tied up in trying to make your partner stay, or in jumping through hoop after hoop for them by showing your unwavering investment, you're being guided by fears of rejection and abandonment (Brown and Elliott 2016; Hazan and Shaver 1987). It is these fears that first need to be addressed and healed, so that you can become more comfortable being truly intimate with your partner.

You may have heard that people who are more avoidantly attached have difficulties with intimacy. It is a pretty common belief that someone who is intimacy avoidant does not want or need a relationship. However, if you are more avoidantly attached, you likely want intimate and close relationships but have chosen autonomy at the expense of closeness with others in your life. This allows you to gain a sense of pseudo-independence, whereby you choose to focus on work or hobbies instead of on interpersonal relationships. Work and hobbies are safer options than risking vulnerability with intimacy. By pushing away intimacy, you are keeping your fear of engulfment in check, at the expense of your intimacy needs (Bartholomew 1990; Brown and Elliott 2016).

Regardless of your attachment style, your intimacy needs *will* collide with your partner's at one time or another. All relationships experience a mismatch in needs every now and then, and this in and of itself should not be seen as a relationship deal-breaker. It's important to recognize a few key points:

First, examine which type of intimacy need you may be experiencing as a perceived mismatch. Are you and your partner not engaging in physical touch or do you wish there was more? Has emotional intimacy reached an impasse? Are you feeling that you and your partner have nothing meaningful to discuss with each other at the end of the day? Could decreases in physical, emotional, or intellectual intimacy be due to hectic work schedules or parenting?

Next, it is important that you take into consideration each of your unique attachment styles and how they influence both of your needs (often on what looks like opposite sides of the coin). However, if you refer back to chapters 2 through 6, hopefully you can reach a richer understanding that what each of you may be needing is not necessarily less or more intimacy but a more solid understanding of *how* your attachment insecurities and intimacy needs may be surfacing.

For example, if you are anxiously attached, you may want or need to feel physically close to your partner when going to sleep by cuddling up to them. Yet, if you are more avoidantly attached, you may want or need personal space for sleep. How can you solve this? It may be as simple as asking your partner to meet you halfway by holding your hand as you fall asleep, then allowing them to have the personal space they need. Or, it may require a little more fine-tuning whereby you each make an effort to prioritize intimacy and explore ways that can work for each of you. Then stick to it.

Prioritizing Intimacy

Prioritizing intimacy can seem awkward and may remove some of the spontaneity. But when you and your partner are prioritizing intimacy in your lives, the goal should be in valuing and meeting each other's needs. Take steps to really get to know each other on a more meaningful level. By prioritizing your and your partner's intimacy needs, it allows for open discussion and can rekindle passion.

For example, you can score double intimacy points by having a deeply connected conversation (for example, focusing on intellectual intimacy needs) while cuddling in bed together (a form of physical intimacy). You might watch a YouTube video together while snuggling, or your partner might open their Kindle and recite something they found interesting from the latest book they are reading while cuddling with you. It is important to recognize the patterns you are noticing within your relationship—whether it is a healthy or anxious-avoidant dynamic—so you and your partner can find a workable solution in building intimacy.

Steps to Building Intimacy

Necessary steps to building intimacy in your relationship include:

1. **Speak your truths to each other.** As a soft start-up, begin by showing gratitude for what you are thankful for regarding intimacy with your partner (Gottman 2015; 1995). Then, openly discuss your intimacy needs and where they are lacking. Use "I" statements, which are often more easily received by others and can lessen any defensiveness between you and your partner. Instead of saying, "You don't sit next to me on the couch when we watch TV," you may try, "I like feeling close to you when we watch TV and want to sit next to you while holding your hand."

2. **Engage in active listening.** Really hear what your partner is saying. Respect that they are allowed to talk while you listen without interruption. This is important in your romantic relationship because your vulnerabilities and feelings are on the line when speaking about your needs.

3. **Self-monitor.** It is always suggested that you consistently self-monitor and recognize if you are becoming tense, angered, or sad in the moment. Take necessary time to allow yourself space to process these feelings safely with your partner when asking for what you need. Take notice of your emotions and body sensations when you speak to your partner. Do you sound confident? Nervous? What is your body language suggesting?

4. **Identify the intimacy need.** It is important to recognize the type of intimacy—emotional, physical, or intellectual—that you are addressing. Label it and then identify

the aspects that you are needing. For example, if you identify that you want more physical intimacy, is it based on proximity and physical closeness to them? Or your partner holding your hand while watching television together? Or something else?

5. **Try simple strategies that can foster intimacy.** Aim for connection while allowing for each partner's attachment needs. Consider ways you can tackle two intimacy needs at once. You do not need elaborate or expensive things to build intimacy. You can try a) holding hands before falling asleep at night as a way of exploring physical intimacy with a more avoidantly attached partner, b) holding hands on a nice walk together and having an intimate conversation (emotional intimacy plus physical intimacy), or c) going to a jazz club together while dancing and chatting about the atmosphere or the music (physical intimacy plus intellectual intimacy).

6. **Be mindful of personal space and time.** Building more meaningful connection and intimacy does not need to extend into all hours of the night, nor should it replace necessary personal time and space for each of you. It is important to recognize that both you and your partner need time to yourselves (we all do), and that time apart should not be seen as threatening or destabilizing to your relationship.

Next, you will start to fine-tune your intimacy needs as well as exploring ways you and your partner can build intimacy.

Establishing and Maintaining Intimacy

PRACTICE EXERCISE

Please take out a pen and a sheet of paper, or your journal, and explore which of the three intimacy needs discussed above you want to focus on. Use the previous steps 1 through 6 as your guide.

Ask your partner to also try the steps on their own.

Then, exchange your answers afterward to gain a richer understanding of each other's needs. Be mindful that their needs may be more aligned with time for personal space, while your needs may appear opposite, or vice versa. Explore a few ways that you both can balance each other's needs for personal space with intimacy.

Now, we will start to integrate everything introduced in the first eight chapters, to help you and your partner build a healthy and fulfilling relationship that lasts.

CHAPTER 9

Fostering Connection and Resolving Differences

After having read the first eight chapters, hopefully you are now feeling more comfortable recognizing how unmet needs, attachment insecurities, and any early environmental trauma can negatively impact and shape your attachment style and your relationship. Attachment insecurities should not make you feel that you are unlovable or that your relationship is doomed to fail. However, when emotional wounds remain unhealed, this is often what happens.

Instead of approaching your relationship from a place of vulnerability and allowing yourself to be fully present, you may be stuck in survival mode, trying to get your unmet needs met. Perhaps you wrongly believe that you are not worthy of receiving love. These kinds of self-defeating messages can be strengthened (reinforced) each time you resort to listening to them, making it that much more difficult to separate yourself from this pattern.

Fortunately, an anxious-avoidant relationship *can* be healed, despite opposing attachment styles between you and your partner. Both of you together can elevate the quality of your connection. However, keep in mind that there is no perfect relationship. If you have been holding out for a partnership that is void of any conflict or differences, one simply does not exist.

The Three C's of Lasting Relationships

There is a lot of information available on what is deemed necessary for a healthy and intimate relationship. For example, you may have heard that chemistry is necessary when choosing a partner. This is true. Chemistry can be explained as a strong physical attraction you feel toward someone and is a catalyst for getting to know them or seeing whether you are a good fit (Sama 2020). Yet, chemistry alone is not sufficient to build or sustain a healthy relationship. Sadly, anyone who has experienced a trauma bond recognizes that relationships only based on intensity, passion, and chemistry are not sustainable. If you are basing your long-term happiness on physical chemistry alone, you are setting yourself up for disappointment once the fireworks fizzle and their looks fade.

Another feature of a healthy romantic relationship is compatibility. Compatibility is necessary for building intimacy between two people, yet it alone is not enough to maintain a healthy bond (Sama 2020). This can be especially true if you or your partner's ideals, worldviews, or goals shift or change during the relationship. Thus, what may have initially attracted you and brought the two of you together based on shared interests may now be a moot point.

Similarly, commitment has also been cited as a necessary element in lasting relationships. It is true that both partners need to be fully committed to each other and the relationship to increase the probability that it will last (Sama 2020). However, commitment alone, without other necessary elements, can lead to *empty love*—a relationship that is void of intimacy and passion (Sternberg 1986). When a relationship is empty, both partners go through the motions of remaining in the relationship, sometimes out of convenience or financial reasons, yet emotional and physical connection are not there.

I believe the most important elements in a healthy relationship are *communication, compromise,* and *consistency.* This is true whether your important relationship is with friends, family, or your partner.

Communication

Communication is one of the most foundational needs of all relationships and involves active listening, mindful engagement, and the ability for each person to safely express their thoughts, feelings, lived experiences, values, and goals in a warm and respectful environment (Sama 2020). Healthy communication is not simply superficial chit-chat; it involves honest feelings on topics that may be triggering to one or both partners. It should also include a safe space in which each person is seen and heard without judgment.

When exploring healthy communication in your relationship, consider the following steps:

- **Respect each other.** Have respect for and validation of each person's reality as worthwhile, even if there is a difference of opinion.

- **Create mindful boundaries.** Always take into consideration boundaries, personal space, and nonverbal communication.

- **Avoid shaming.** Each person should hold their own perspectives and feelings without fear of being shamed.

- **Aim to be solution-focused.** Resolve conflict with solution-focused goals in mind.

When communication suffers, either from communication excesses or deficits (see chapter 4), it may cause a breakdown in overall intimacy and create an environment ripe for resentment.

Compromise

Chances are, you and your partner will not be perfectly in agreement on everything in your relationship (Sama 2020). What may be important to you may not be as important to them, and vice versa. Differences in priorities, needs, desires, or feelings can leave you both choosing your own perspectives while downplaying the other person's. Thus, taking the time to compromise can help you reach a mutual agreement on each other's opposing viewpoints by splitting any differences down the middle.

For example, if you are a beach lover and your partner is a mountain lover, you may reach a compromise with your vacation plans by agreeing to visit each spot or visiting one location now and the other on your next vacation. On a deeper level, healthy compromising may include how much time to spend with in-laws, friends, or extended family during the holidays or reunions. It may include issues surrounding planning for having children, work-life balance, or how to best support each other if one partner develops depression or other mental health challenge.

Of course, compromising on what will be mutually agreeable for both of you also means that you and your partner will not resort to passive-aggressive tactics.

Comprising should not be confused with *surrendering*. Healthy compromise is based on mutuality, whereby you and your partner meet in the middle on something and are both satisfied with a doable outcome. Unlike compromise, surrendering is one-sided and selfish; you or your partner consistently give up your desires, choices, or needs by trying to keep the peace. If you or your partner are resorting to surrendering your needs for the sake of maintaining your relationship, take note that these are signs of people-pleasing behavior and self-betrayal, not compromise.

When exploring healthy compromise in your relationship, adhere to the following guidelines:

- **Validate.** Make sure that you both feel seen, heard, appreciated, and understood in asking for and reaching a compromise.

- **Avoid manipulation.** For example, don't give up your feelings or needs so you can hold it over your partner's head.

- **Ensure a balance of power.** Aim for an equal balance of power between you and your partner that is void of threats or passive-aggressive tactics.

- **Share freely.** Open the doors for deeper communication and intimacy whenever exploring a compromise.

Consistency

Consistency is one of the most critical elements of a healthy and connected romantic relationship. Yet, it is also one of the most overlooked and neglected foundational qualities when it comes to cultivating healthy relationships. Consistency is a necessary safety need that begins in childhood and should be taught and modeled from emotionally mature and present caregivers (see chapter 5). Yet, if what you learned was inconsistency, this pattern resonates with a lack of follow-through. You may not recognize *why* you change your thoughts, feelings, needs, or patterns. Consistent behavior in your romantic relationship includes unpacking your motivations for holding certain routines, repetitive patterns, or beliefs. Consistency is aligned with word and deed, whereas inconsistency equates to saying one thing while doing another.

If there are inconsistencies in your relationship, you may not be aware of what motivates you to hold certain beliefs about your partner or how you behave toward them. Ideally, if you and your partner are consistent in your behavior, your thoughts and feelings will be aligned with your actions. You and your partner will be able to show up for yourselves and each other.

When working to establish consistency in your relationship, try the following guidelines:

- **Establish structure.** Provide yourselves and each other a sense of day-to-day continuity, structure, routine, and stability.

- **Align speech and action.** Ensure there is no hypocrisy or mismatch between what you and your partner say versus what each of you does.

- **Check expectations.** Show up for each other and the relationship without expectations or incentives of something being in it for you.

- **Be consistent.** Make sure that feelings, thoughts, attitudes, beliefs, and behaviors are patterned, dependable, and lacking in impulsivity.

Now, take a moment to explore what you just read about the three C's of lasting relationships when completing the next exercise.

Fostering Connection and Resolving Differences

PRACTICE EXERCISE

The three C's of lasting relationships can be a gauge of whether each of you is providing the other communication, compromise, and consistency. This exercise can help you both continue building these necessary skills. Please grab your pen and paper, or your journal, and respond to the following prompts. At the end of the exercise, you'll find the answer key.

Read this short vignette and take the quiz that follows. *Steve and Brittany have been in a romantic relationship for a few years. According to Brittany, their relationship started out "hot and heavy." But over the last year or so, she began feeling disconnected from Steve, as if he were a stranger. Brittany has tried bringing this up to Steve on a few occasions, but each time she tries, he ends up talking for her, only seeing his perspective, rolling his eyes at her, and becoming confrontational. He is becoming more difficult to talk to and resorts to jumping on his phone or walking out of the room when she tries expressing her needs.*

1. Steve's communication style appears to be lacking:

   a. Respect for and validation of Brittany's reality as worthwhile, even if he has a difference of opinion

   b. Boundaries, personal space, and nonverbal communication that are healthy, receptive, and welcoming for each person involved

   c. Holding space for Brittany's feelings without shaming or belittling her

   d. Healthy conflict resolution with solution-focused goals in mind

   e. All of the above.

2. Explore what Steve and Brittany could do from chapter 8 to help build intimacy within their relationship. What could Steve also do to build a healthier way of communicating with Brittany?

3. Free-write in your journal about which one of the three C's—communication, compromise, or consistency—you feel is most important in your romantic relationship and why. Ask your partner to do the same.

4. Then, refer to "Steps to Building Intimacy" in chapter 8. Explore the type of intimacy you can cultivate based on whether you chose communication, compromise, or consistency. For example, if you chose consistency as most important for you, how can consistency be applied to building experiences that are emotionally intimate? Physically intimate? Intellectually Intimate? Ask your partner to do the same.

5. Share your responses with each other.

Answer key

1. E, all of the above. Steve seems to have violated each of the four elements necessary for healthy communication. This becomes evident in how he treats Brittany when she tries talking about her intimacy needs.

2. Answers could include the different types of intimacy explored in chapter 8, as well as considering how secure their relationship is. Brittany may be describing a high level of chemistry early in the relationship with the reference to "hot and heavy." She may need to explore if there are deeper needs being met, such as authentic compatibility or consistency within the relationship. This may also include Brittany keeping track of how many times she tries communicating with Steve about her needs along with his reactions to her requests. She may try tallying the frequency and intensity of each argument, along with exploring one or two solutions together. However, if Steve continues to downplay Brittany's emotional needs without a solution being found, or if his behavior is more

narcissistic, Brittany will need to reevaluate her needs, which may include leaving the relationship for her own mental, emotional, and physical health.

The Four R's for Resolving Differences

As you and your partner work on your relationship, differences and disagreements are likely to come up at one time or another. This is where effective resolutions can come in handy. I call them the four R's for resolving differences: *recognition, redirection, reflection,* and *reconnection.* These four R's are very flexible and can adapt to various situations and relationship dynamics, including strengthening the relationships you have with your partner and yourself.

The R's can be an excellent way to help both partners in becoming more flexible with conflict resolution and building intimacy. They work together as behavioral supports for couples who are seeking ways to foster a deeper connection. They can be used with relationships that are already healthy and secure, and with push-pull dynamics wherein a couple is addressing intimacy needs, communication differences, or attachment insecurities.

First, you'll discover what each of these steps include. Next, you will consider how to start unpacking each step. Finally, you will read another vignette of a couple experiencing an anxious-avoidant relationship and gain insight into how they can successfully use the four R's in deescalating conflict and building intimacy.

Recognition

Recognition of something means you have awareness of it. Awareness is a critical first step for any type of behavior change, because without actually seeing or recognizing that something may be off between you and your partner, jumping headfirst into trying to fix the situation will be futile.

Recognition includes two distinct but interconnected parts: *self-awareness* and *relationship awareness*. By first building self-awareness, you are building a mental checklist of your own patterns and triggers. Part of building self-awareness also includes recognizing that what may be triggering to you may not be triggering to your partner, and vice versa. Thus, it is important to become aware of certain themes, topics, and events that cause you to impulsively react instead of respond (Budzan and Van Vliet 2021).

For example, by gaining deeper self-awareness, you may notice that discussions about finances or going over to your in-laws' house on the weekend are triggering topics for you that often lead to an argument. Self-awareness requires that you are receptive to wanting to understand yourself on a deeper level, including any attachment insecurities. It includes being open to honestly examining your verbal and nonverbal behavior during a disagreement, whether you became defensive, shut down, lash out, or criticize your partner. It involves noticing what you may be thinking or feeling. Self-awareness can also include keeping track of the frequency and intensity of arguments, along with any threats to intimacy and communication that may be unfolding (see chapters 7 and 8).

Similarly, *relationship awareness* can include recognizing and acknowledging differences in how you and your partner respond to each other. It is about being mindful of each other's verbal and non-verbal communication, along with triggering topics that typically result in a disagreement. Relationship awareness also includes taking stock of the common traits of an anxious-avoidant relationship and identifying which ones represent patterns seen between you and your partner (see chapter 8).

Fostering Connection and Resolving Differences

Redirection

Redirection is when you choose to place your energy into something that is less emotionally triggering or unproductive. It involves choosing healthier ways of responding. Once you gain more self-awareness in recognizing your emotional triggers, you can then proactively learn to redirect your actions to something more mindful to deescalate or prevent an argument.

For example, if discussions about finances usually lead to becoming defensive or lashing out at your partner when they bring up bills, you may also start recognizing how you become defensive or what you say when lashing out. This recognition can allow you the space and necessary time to redirect your actions to a healthier alternative. For instance, you can instead ask for a few minutes to yourself or reach a compromise with your partner that finances will only be discussed at the beginning or end of each month.

It should be noted that it is common to confuse *avoiding* something with redirecting your behavior to something else. The two are not the same. Avoidance behaviors are maladaptive coping strategies whereby you tune out or pretend that something you don't want to deal with is not there. Redirection involves recognizing what caused you to have an emotional reaction and then engaging in a healthier response. For example, an avoidance behavior may look like asking your partner to discuss finances later, and then continuing to dodge the conversation each time they bring it up. A redirected behavior may include setting a place and time to discuss finances, and then sticking to it.

Reflection

Self-reflection is a necessary self-discovery process that both you and your partner need to assess your actions, motivations, feelings, and needs surrounding any disagreements (Gottman 2015). When you allow yourself time to process and examine your actions or reactions, you are also taking steps toward emotional growth. While this may not always be easy to do, when you reflect on your decisions and actions, you can gain insight into your motivations and unmet needs. Additionally, by allowing your partner personal space to sort through their needs, you are giving them necessary time for their own improved self-awareness and decision-making process.

With self-reflection, you are taking necessary steps in unpacking emotional insecurities that may be overshadowing your ability to respond in a healthier way. Self-reflection could include journaling, which can help you make deeper connections between your triggers and your reactions. For example, through journaling, you may come to recognize that talking about finances with your partner is triggering to you because of having grown up in poverty. From this process, you may discover that it is not your partner bringing up finances that is triggering as much as it is your insecurities surrounding your early environment. With this newfound awareness, you can then take steps in your emotional healing.

Reconnection

Reconnection is the final step. It includes both you and your partner each taking necessary time to speak your truth about your feelings, needs, and possible solutions regarding any issues within your relationship so you can both reconnect emotionally (Gottman 2015). When you and your partner reconnect, you each openly communicate your needs. You get to share insights gained regarding each of your needs, identify relationship strengths, and provide each other possible solutions regarding relationship challenges.

Reconnection should include healthy communication skills, such as being mindful of allowing each person to speak uninterrupted and respecting personal boundaries. Reconnection involves both partners being understanding of the other's perspective, even if it differs from their own. Because the goal of reconnecting is to allow each partner to openly communicate about what they learned through self-discovery and self-reflection, it is important that each person use "I" statements when discussing their feelings or the things that they want to discuss. Reconnection is not about drudging up past arguments.

Now, you'll turn your attention to another vignette about a couple who is experiencing some common issues within an anxious-avoidant relationship. See if you can unpack ways that they may use the four R's in supporting their relationship.

• *Pete and Brian*

Pete and Brian both love nature and the mountains. About five years ago, they invested in a large cabin and did a beautiful remodel on it. They spend most weekends and the entire winter there because Brian loves the snow. While neither minds packing up and hustling to get to the cabin to relax, Pete usually resorts to workaholic behavior once they settle in. The first thing he does is turn on his laptop, lie on the floor, and begin to work—which can go on for hours.

Brian and Pete have gotten into some heated arguments over the years about how Pete cannot seem to disconnect from his job, run errands with Brian, or help around the cabin. Brian says that Pete seems more interested in work than being around nature or the man who loves him. Brian also admits he has started arguments with Pete because he feels that he is spending more time on his laptop than with him. He denies becoming clingy when trying to get Pete's attention, although Pete has mentioned this to him on numerous occasions when Brian passive-aggressively stands in front of his laptop to pull him away from his work.

Pete tries reassuring Brian by stating that he is responsible for employee regulations and the company's website, which takes up a lot of time. However, Pete also admits that he often feels overwhelmed with Brian demanding more and more of his time, knowing he has work to do. Pete says that work has been an escape for him and helps him decompress from the relationship stress.

Brian usually goes for a hike and leaves Pete in the cabin. Brian admits he has become angrier toward Pete. Brian now has mixed feelings about his relationship and questions whether Pete values his job more than him. What used to be a wonderful escape from the city has turned into tension and loneliness for Brian and frustration for Pete. They are both at a stalemate as to what to do.

Now, let's take a moment to unpack Brian and Pete's story. As you look at their relationship, notice how you can become more comfortable using the four R's and other tools in your own relationship.

Both Pete and Brian have a decent amount of self-awareness and relationship awareness (forms of *recognition*). For example, they both recognize that they love spending time in the mountains together, have worked very hard to afford this lifestyle, and are aware that they are at a stalemate in how to move past arguing. Brian recognizes that he has started arguments with Pete over his workaholism and that he has become passive-aggressive and angry toward Pete. However, Brian seems to have a blind spot when it comes to recognizing his actions toward Pete that may be considered clingy or demanding, such as standing in front of his laptop and demanding more of his time. Similarly, Pete may have a blind spot when it comes to how much he is excessively working, although he did mention that work offers him a respite from the stress with Brian.

With regard to *redirection*, Brian engages in the healthier option of going out for a hike instead of demanding more of Pete's time. However, Brian needs to address any anger or passive-aggression, so that going out for a hike doesn't upset Pete or cause a further breakdown in communication.

Brian can use his hikes proactively as a way of tapping into his own self-discovery process through *reflection*. This can also allow him time to unpack any early wounds, such as environmental or attachment insecurities stemming from his childhood, fear of intimacy, unmet safety or belonging needs, or any patterns of unhealthy responding (see chapters 2 through 6). For example, through the process of self-reflection, Brian may discover that he is more anxiously attached, fears that Pete will abandon him for his career, and ultimately feels unseen and unheard in the relationship.

However, for Pete to begin self-reflection, he would have to allow himself time away from his workaholism. A good place for him to start the self-discovery process may be through journaling and tapping into how many hours he works a week, when it started, and what his motivations are in working so much. He may discover that work has been a distraction for him and gives him the necessary space he needs. Through this realization, Pete may recognize that he is more avoidantly attached. As Pete continues his exploration, he may uncover that his workaholism is tied to a need to be seen as perfect, stemming from his narcissistic parents who disapproved of him and made him feel as if he was never good enough.

As Pete and Brian continue with their insights, they are primed for *reconnection*. During reconnection, they may want to use the skills of healthier communication, such as active listening and respecting the other person's needs. For example, they could discuss ways they can work on balancing intimacy with personal space (chapter 8). They can also explore ways to reach a compromise with Pete's work schedule. It is important that both Brian and Pete respect each other's perspectives and possible differences in opinions while remaining on target with the issue at hand.

In the exercises that follows, you'll be given a chance to explore the four R's of resolving differences in your relationship.

PRACTICE EXERCISE

In this exercise, you will be writing down your personal relationship story. You can use Brian and Pete's vignette as an example.

1. Grab your journal or a pen and paper.

2. Describe one situation that is triggering to you and has caused repeated stress and tension in your relationship.

3. After you have completed your personal story, use the four R's for resolving differences, discussed in this chapter, to analyze your vignette. Be sure to include how often you and your partner argue about the issue, the average intensity of these arguments, and a couple of proposed solutions (see chapter 8).

4. Include ways you and your partner can cultivate more intimacy emotionally, physically, and intellectually. Also include which of the C's—communication, compromise, or consistency—you feel is most necessary in helping to resolve the relationship issue and build lasting connection with your partner (see earlier in chapter 9).

Breaking Free from the Anxious-Avoidant Trap

Congratulations in choosing your empowerment and relationship success! Each step you and your partner continue taking together is one step closer to a relationship that is emotionally fulfilling, connected, and intimate. Each moment you both pause, reflect, and choose to use the tools outlined in this book, you are continuing to create space for a relationship that fosters healthy communication, respect for each other's individual needs, and a deeper understanding of each other.

Fostering Connection and Resolving Differences

It is my hope that you both see the beauty in your uniqueness and that your "differences" really aren't that different. It is in learning to recognize the areas in your relationship where change is needed that you both can continue taking strides in mastering those changes. My goal for you is that you both approach your relationship from a new and healthier perspective—one that considers each of your individual needs and the love you share.

As you both embark on a more satisfying relationship together, remember that growth is a process—and one that requires self-compassion and patience. You chose each other for a reason! Trust that you are creating a relationship that is a reflection of your continued growth.

References

Bakwin, M. W. 1942. "Loneliness in Infants." *Archives of Pediatrics & Adolescent Medicine* 63(1): 30–40.

Bartholomew, K. 1990. "Avoidance of Intimacy: An Attachment Perspective." *Journal of Social and Personal Relationships* 7(2): 147–178.

Bosmans, G., Bakermans-Kranenburg, M. J., Vervliet, V., Verhees, M. W. F. T., and Van Ijzendoorn, M. H. 2020. "A Learning Theory of Attachment: Unraveling the Black Box of Attachment Development." *Neuroscience and Biobehavioral Reviews* 113: 287–298.

Bowlby, J. 1969. *Attachment and Loss* Volume I. New York: Basic Books.

Brown, D. P., and Elliott, D. S. 2016. *Attachment Disturbances: Treatment for Comprehensive Repair.* New York: W.W. Norton.

Budzan, B. N., and Van Vliet, K. J. 2021. "The Influence of a Self-Compassion Training Program on Romantic Relationship Conflict: An Exploratory Multiple-Case Study." *Canadian Journal of Counseling and Psychotherapy* 55(3): 315-333.

Campbell, W. K., and Miller, J. D. 2011. *The Handbook of Narcissism and Narcissistic Personality Disorder: Theoretical Approaches, Empirical Findings, and Treatments.* Hoboken, NJ: John Wiley & Sons.

Cassidy, J., and Kobak, R. R. 1988. "Avoidance and Its Relationship with Other Defensive Processes." In *Clinical Implications of Attachment*, edited by J. Belsky and T. Nezworski. Hillsdale, NJ: Erlbaum.

Carmo, C., Oliveira, D., Bras, M., and Faisca, L. 2021. "The Influence of Parental Perfectionism and Parenting Styles on Child Perfectionism." *Children* 8(9): 1–11.

Chapman, G. D. 2010. *The Five Love Languages*. Farmington Hills: Walker Large Print.

Collins, N. L., and Read, S. J. 1990. "Adult Attachment, Working Models of Relationship Quality in Dating Couples." *Journal of Personality and Social Psychology* 58(4): 644–663.

Cruz, D., Lichten, M., Berg, K., and George, P. 2022. "Developmental Trauma: Conceptual Framework, Associated Risks and Comorbidities, and Evaluation and Treatment." *Frontiers in Psychiatry* 13: 800687.

Doron, G., Moulding, R., Kyrios, M., and Nedeljkovic, M. 2009. "Adult Attachment Insecurities Are Related to Obsessive Compulsive Phenomena." *Journal of Social and Clinical Psychology* 28(8): 1,022–1,049.

Dutton, D. G., and Painter, S. 1993. "Emotional Attachments in Abusive Relationships: A Test of Traumatic Bonding Theory." *Violence and Victims* 8(2): 105–120.

Gottman, J. M., and Silver, N. 2015. *The Seven Principles for Making Marriage Work: A Practical Guide from the Country's Foremost Relationship Expert*. New York: Harmony.

Gottman, J. M., and Silver, N. 1995. *Why Marriages Succeed or Fail: And How You Can Make Yours Last*. New York: Simon & Schuster.

References

Harlow, H. F. 1958. "The Nature of Love." *American Psychologist* 13(12): 673–685.

Hazan, C., and Shaver, P. R. 1987. "Romantic Love Conceptualized as an Attachment Process." *Journal of Personality and Social Psychology* 52: 511–524.

Kermanian, S., Golshani, F., Baghdasarians, A., and Jomhari, F. 2021. "The Mediating Role of Perfectionism in Relation to Narcissism and Trauma, Family Functioning, and Perceived Parenting Styles." *Journal of Community Health Research* 10(2): 117–127.

Kernberg, O. F. 1985. *Borderline Conditions and Pathological Narcissism.* Lanham, MD: Rowman & Littlefield.

Levine, A., and Heller, R. 2010. *Attached: The New Science of Adult Attachment and How It Can Help You Find—and Keep—Love.* New York: Penguin.

Lozano, L. M., Segura-Valor, I., Garcia-Cueto, E., Pedrose, I., Llanos, A., and Lozano, L. 2019. "Relationship Between Child Perfectionism and Psychological Disorders." *Frontiers in Psychology* 10: 1–7.

Macfie, J., McElwain, N. I., Houts, R. M., and Cox, M. J. 2005. "Intergenerational Transmission of Role Reversal Between Parent and Child: Dyadic and Family Systems Internal Working Models." *Attachment & Human Development* 7(1): 51–65.

Mahoney, D. M., Rickspoone, L., and Hull, J. C. 2016. "Narcissism, Parenting, Complex Trauma: The Emotional Consequences for Children by Narcissistic Parents." *Journal of Counseling and Professional Psychology* 5: 45–60.

Main, M. 2000. "The Organized Categories of Infant, Child, and Adult Attachment: Flexible vs. Inflexible Attention

Under Attachment-Related Stress." *Journal of the American Psychoanalytic* 48(4): 1,055–1,096.

Main, M. 1990. "Cross-Cultural Studies of Attachment Organization: Recent Studies, Changing Methodologies, and the Concept of Conditional Strategies." *Human Development* 33: 48–61.

Main, M., and Hesse, E. 1990. "Parents' Unresolved Traumatic Experiences Are Related to Infant Disorganized Attachment Status: Is Frightened and/or Frightening Parental Behavior the Linking Mechanism?" In M. T. Greenberg, D. Cicchetti, and E. M. Cummings (Eds.), *Attachment in the Preschool Years: Theory, Research, and Intervention* (pp. 161–182). Chicago: University of Chicago Press.

Maslow, A. 1943. "A Theory of Human Motivation." *Psychological Review* 50: 370–396.

Maslow, A. H. 1962. *Toward a Psychology of Being.* New York: Harper.

Maslow, A. H., and Frager, R. 1987. *Motivation and Personality,* 3rd ed. New York: Harper and Row.

Minuchin, S. 1974. *Families and Family Therapy.* London: Routledge.

Mortazavizadeh, Z., Gollner, L., and Forstmeier, S. 2022. "Emotional Competence, Attachment, and Parenting Styles in Children and Parents." *Psicologia: Reflexão e Crítica* 35(6): 1–12.

Mukilincer, M. 2007. *Attachment in Adulthood: Structure, Dynamics, and Change.* New York: Guilford Press.

Mukilincer, M., and Shaver, P. 2003. "The Attachment Behavioral System in Adulthood: Activation, Psychodynamics, and Impersonal Processes." In *Advances in Experimental Social Psychology,* edited by M. P. Zanna. New York: Academic Press.

Rholes, W. S., Simpson, J. A., Tran, S., Martin, A. M., and Friedman, M. 2007. "Attachment and Information Seeking in Romantic Relationships." *Personality and Social Psychology Bulletin* 33(3): 422–438.

Rholes, W. S. and Simpson, J. A. 2004. *Adult Attachment: Theory, Research, and Clinical Implications*. New York: Guilford Press.

Sama, J. M. 2020. "The 5 C's of Every Healthy Relationship." *James M Sama*, April 7. https://jamesmsama.com/2020/04/07 /the-5-cs-of-every-healthy-relationship/.

Schienle, A., Wabnegger, A., Schongassner, F., and Leutgeb, V. 2015. "Effects of Personal Space Intrusion in Affective Contexts: An fMRI Investigation with Women Suffering from Borderline Personality Disorder." *Social Cognitive and Affective Neuroscience* 10(10): 1,424–1,428.

Simpson, J. A., Kim, J. S., Fillo, J., Ickes, W., Rholes, W. S., Onna, M. M., and Winterheld, H. A. 2011. "Attachment and the Management of Empathetic Accuracy in Relationship-Threatening Situations." *Personality and Social Psychology* 37(2): 242–254.

Sternberg, R. J. 1986. "A Triangular Theory of Love." *Psychological Review* 93: 119–135.

Tanasugarn, A. 2022. "How Childhood Invalidation Affects Adult Well-being." *Psychology Today*. https://www.psychologytoday .com/us/blog/understanding-ptsd/202207/how-childhood -invalidation-affects-adult-well-being.

Wei, M., Mallinckrodt, B., Larson, L. M., and Zakalik, R. A. 2005. "Adult Attachment, Depressive Symptoms, and Validation from Self Versus Others." *Journal of Counseling Psychology* 52(3): 368–377.

Annie Tanasugarn, PhD, is a relationship specialist who coaches highly motivated individuals in improving their emotional well-being and building healthier, more fulfilling relationships. With a deep understanding of the impact of past experiences on current behavior, she offers meaningful programs designed to support clients in overcoming toxic relationship challenges, breaking free from negative patterns, and fostering personal growth. Through a combination of actionable tools and a compassionate approach, she empowers clients to develop greater self-awareness, emotional resilience, and stronger connections with themselves and others.

Real change *is* possible

For more than fifty years, New Harbinger has published proven-effective self-help books and pioneering workbooks to help readers of all ages and backgrounds improve mental health and well-being, and achieve lasting personal growth. In addition, our spirituality books offer profound guidance for deepening awareness and cultivating healing, self-discovery, and fulfillment.

Founded by psychologist Matthew McKay and Patrick Fanning, New Harbinger is proud to be an independent, employee-owned company. Our books reflect our core values of integrity, innovation, commitment, sustainability, compassion, and trust. Written by leaders in the field and recommended by therapists worldwide, New Harbinger books are practical, accessible, and provide real tools for real change.

 newharbingerpublications

MORE BOOKS from NEW HARBINGER PUBLICATIONS

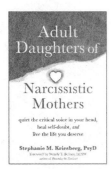

ADULT DAUGHTERS OF NARCISSISTIC MOTHERS

Quiet the Critical Voice in Your Head, Heal Self-Doubt, and Live the Life You Deserve

978-1648480096 / US $18.95

WIRED FOR LOVE, SECOND EDITION

How Understanding Your Partner's Brain and Attachment Style Can Help You Defuse Conflict and Build a Secure Relationship

978-1648482960 / US $19.95

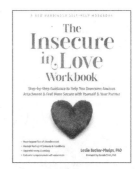

THE INSECURE IN LOVE WORKBOOK

Step-by-Step Guidance to Help You Overcome Anxious Attachment and Feel More Secure with Yourself and Your Partner

978-1648482175 / US $25.95

HEALING THE TRAUMA OF INFIDELITY

Powerful Skills for Rebuilding Trust and Attachment to Find Love, Commitment, and Intimacy Again

978-1648485725 / US $19.95

THE HIGHLY SENSITIVE PERSON'S GUIDE TO DEALING WITH TOXIC PEOPLE

How to Reclaim Your Power from Narcissists and Other Manipulators

978-1684035304 / US $20.95

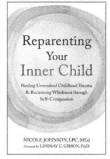

REPARENTING YOUR INNER CHILD

Healing Unresolved Childhood Trauma and Reclaiming Wholeness through Self-Compassion

978-1648485091 / US $19.95

newharbingerpublications

1-800-748-6243 / newharbinger.com

(VISA, MC, AMEX / prices subject to change without notice)

Follow Us

Don't miss out on new books from New Harbinger.
Subscribe to our email list at **newharbinger.com/subscribe**